CALLED *to* CONQUER

Books Available from Derek Prince Ministries

Appointment in Jerusalem
Atonement: Your Appointment
    with God
Blessing or Curse: You Can
Choose
Choice of a Partner, The
Complete Salvation
Declaring God's Word
Derek Prince—A Biography by
    Stephen Mansfield
Derek Prince: On Experiencing
    God's Power
Destiny Of Israel and The Church,
Divine Exchange, The
Does Your Tongue Need Healing?
End of Life's Journey, The
Entering the Presence of God
Expelling Demons
Explaining Blessings and Curses
Extravagant Love
Faith to Live By
Fasting
First Mile, The
Foundations For Christian Living
Gateway to God's Blessing
Gifts of the Spirit, The
God Is a Matchmaker
God's Medicine Bottle
God's Plan for Your Money
God's Remedy for Rejection
God's Will for Your Life
God's Word Heals
Grace of Yielding, The
Holy Spirit in You, The
How to Fast Successfully
Husbands and Fathers

I Forgive You
Judging
Life's Bitter Pool
Lucifer Exposed
Marriage Covenant, The
Orphans, Widows, the Poor
    and Oppressed
Our Debt to Israel
Pages from My Life's Book
Partners for Life
Philosophy, the Bible and the
    Supernatural
Power in the Name
Power of the Sacrifice, The
Prayers and Proclamations
Praying for the Government
Protection from Deception
Promised Land
Prophetic Guide to the End Times
Receiving God's Best
Rediscovering God's Church
Rules of Engagement
Secrets of a Prayer Warrior
Self-Study Bible Course
    (revised and expanded)
Shaping History Through Prayer
    and Fasting
Spiritual Warfare
Surviving the Last Days
They Shall Expel Demons
Through the Psalms with
    Derek Prince
War in Heaven
Who Is the Holy Spirit?
You Matter to God
You Shall Receive Power

CALLED *to* CONQUER

Finding Your Assignment
in the
Kingdom of God

DEREK PRINCE

Published by DPM-UK
Kingsfield, Hadrian Way
Baldock, Herts, SG7 6AN
www.dpmuk.org

ISBN: 978-1-901144-57-4
Product Code: B89

This book was compiled from the extensive archive of Derek Prince's unpublished materials and edited by the Derek Prince Ministries editorial team.

Derek Prince Ministries
www.derekprince.com

Contents

Foreword

I believe there are two great moments in a person's life. The first is the moment you were born. The second is the moment you discover *why* you were born.

We are all born for a reason, and it is our responsibility to discover that reason—the "why," the *Calling*, of our lives. Then we can redirect our path toward God's optimal purpose for our lives. It is when you reach this second moment that your life—your Calling—starts to take shape.

Yet many of us miss this, and we live in a perpetual state of survival, of shallowness, of conformity. We forget, deny or never take the time to realize what we were truly born to do. We turn to parents, family, popular culture, want ads or maybe even the path of least resistance to tell us what would make our lives valuable. We wait for a divine voice to boom from the clouds, "You there! Yes, you! This is what I am calling you to do!"

But that is not how it works. You need to take action. And when you do, your life will never be the same.

If you want to turn an ordinary life into an extraordinary one, you have to take the first step. It starts with a single recognition. Your Calling is given to you at birth. But you need to discover it like a treasure, recognizing it for the significance it possesses.

I'm not talking strictly about a spiritual calling or only finding your spiritual gifts. I'm talking about a total reawakening, a full realization of your full potential in every aspect of your life. Think of a lunar eclipse. In one perfect moment, the sun and moon align to create a wonder of nature. A Calling is like that. It is the optimal alignment of your mind, body and spirit with God's primary purpose for your life.

When this happens, something "clicks" within you, and you know you have found what you were created to do. It is an instinctive, gut-level, spiritual experience. You'll know it when you see, hear and feel it.

Derek Prince was a man who knew his Calling. Educated at the most prestigious academic institutions, he spoke numerous languages and was schooled in both ancient and modern philosophy. Yet it was not until he was serving with the British army in World War II that he received his ultimate marching orders: to preach the Word of God to all in a simple way, making it accessible for everyone to understand.

His life was changed by his discovery. Suddenly he found himself on a completely different trajectory than he had ever envisioned while pursuing his earlier academic career. Yet Derek was faithful to his Calling, and his legacy is evidence of this. Countless lives have been changed and blessed by his ultimate obedience to the Lord and the Lord's plan for him.

You picked up this book for a reason. Like Derek, you feel that pull deep down in your soul. The pull to something greater—something better than what you have right now. You might have a perfect life on paper: a loving spouse, obedient kids, a comfortable home, a high-paying job, the cars and clothes that draw stares of envy. Or you might not have any of that and are left with empty hands wondering, *What am I here for?*

Wherever you are right now, you picked up this book because you feel a stirring inside of you to live a life of divine importance. Yet somehow, you are not able to put into words what that importance is or what it is supposed to look like. You need a guide, a helper, a friend, to walk you through this process of discovery. And I can't think of a better person to come alongside you than Derek Prince.

Contained in this book is a wealth of simple, solid guidance from a life lived inside God's plan. Not only will Derek's words help you discover God's Calling, they will also equip you to realign your path to follow the one God has laid out for you.

Remember: You have to know your mission before you accomplish it. May the Lord bless you as you read these pages, and may you seek, find and fulfill His Calling for your life.

Pastor Kirbyjon Caldwell
Windsor Village Methodist Church
Houston, Texas

1

The Upward Call

Jesus, walking by the Sea of Galilee, saw two brothers, Simon called Peter, and Andrew his brother, casting a net into the sea; for they were fishermen. Then He said to them, "Follow Me, and I will make you fishers of men." They immediately left their nets and followed Him. Going on from there, He saw two other brothers, James . . . and John . . . in the boat with Zebedee their father, mending their nets. He called them, and immediately they left the boat and their father, and followed Him.

MATTHEW 4:18–22

I find it interesting that the first four men Jesus called were fishermen. In some measure, I think I understand the wisdom of God in His choice. Fishermen are a breed apart. If you are reading this and you are a fisherman, you know that fishermen are fanatics.

Sometimes when I have gone for a walk, I have passed by men who are fishing. I notice that the fish are not biting. But then I think, *That doesn't matter—they're fishermen.* Circumstances never bother them. Discouragement never affects them. Adverse weather is not a problem for them. They have a vision for fish.

The Lord gave us a wonderful message when He began His ministry with fishermen: Christians should be like that. We should be so passionate about answering His call that nothing else matters.

Notice, too, that Jesus did not waste a lot of words in calling His disciples: "Follow Me." This may be the shortest sermon on record! As we will discover, He did not—and does not—do a great deal of explaining. This shows us that there is no compromise in this commitment to Jesus. There is no middle ground.

> Jesus said to His disciples, "If anyone desires to come after Me, let him deny himself, and take up his cross, and follow Me. For whoever desires to save his life will lose it, but whoever loses his life for My sake will find it."
>
> Matthew 16:24–25

Later in His ministry Jesus gave this same call to another man: "Follow Me." The man hesitated. "Lord, let me first go and bury my father." Jesus replied, "Let the dead bury their own dead, but you go and preach the Kingdom of God" (see Luke 9:59–60). When Jesus says, "Now," tomorrow is not good enough. He challenges us directly and lets us decide how we will answer Him.

I grew up in the Anglican Church in Britain, and I was a member for the first part of my life. They made it pretty easy to belong (as many churches do) by saying, "You don't have to do much, but you do have to do just these few things." I did all the things that I was supposed to do, but I never found reality in my life.

At the time, I did not know my own heart, but what I was looking for was a challenge. The first time I was confronted by the challenge of Jesus, I responded with total commitment. I suspect that many other people have not grown too excited by conventional religion. They are not fully satisfied, but they do not know what would satisfy them. I want to suggest that what they are looking for is the challenge of the unequivocal, uncompromising call of God. If you receive that call, do not let anything keep you back from the excitement of responding.

God's call is holy and it is heavenly. It is an upward call. It is as if we move along a horizontal plane, and God's vertical call comes from heaven and bisects our lives. Our lives before His call are quite different from what our lives become if we respond to that call.

You can save your life if you hold onto it. You can keep it for yourself, please yourself, make your own plans, do what you want to do, but you will lose your life. Or, you can lay it down—and you will find another. In His authority and sovereignty He says simply, "Follow Me." That's all.

Sovereignty is somewhat a theological word. I interpret it this way: God does *what* He wants *when* He wants the *way* He wants, and He *asks no one's permission.* This idea of His sovereignty, which has been largely neglected in this present generation, is one of the great truths of Scripture. Until we appreciate and honor God's sovereignty, we will be unable to understand His call on our lives. But if we are willing to go forward with that understanding, we will enter the new life—with all of its benefits. Here are just four aspects.

Do You Want to Enter "Forever"?

Our motivation in pursuing the new life is, at its simplest, the desire to do the will of God. That was the motivation of Jesus Himself. He said, "My food is to do the will of Him who sent Me, and to finish His work" (John 4:34).

In his first epistle, John speaks about the one who does the will of God. He contrasts that with everything this world has to offer. John clearly says, "The world is passing away, and the lust of it" (1 John 2:17). All the world's desires and ambitions, everything it grasps for and strives after are all temporary. They are all going to pass away.

After this initial statement, however, is the word *but*: "But he who does the will of God abides forever" (1 John 2:17). That is the difference. When you renounce your own will, when you say no to yourself and unite your will with God's will, you meet the conditions.

In the last resort, God's will is going to be done. If you become identified with His will, you become unsinkable, undefeatable. You are going to last forever. Isn't that exciting? I invite you to make that proclamation in a little more personal manner, like this: "If I do the will of God, I will abide forever."

That is the first mark of the new life. It is a life united to the will of God. It has in it all the strength, power and confidence of God's own will.

Do You Want Perfect Guidance?

The new life is also one that is directed by the Holy Spirit. Let's look at just one verse of Scripture: "As many as are led by the Spirit of God, these are sons of God" (Romans 8:14).

This verse is all in the continuing present tense. Another way to phrase it is: As many as are regularly led by the Spirit of God, these are sons of God. When you receive Jesus as your personal Savior by faith, you are born of the Spirit of God. You become a tiny infant in God's family. But to grow up into a mature son or daughter in His Kingdom, there is a further process: being led by the Spirit of God. Many Christians who have been born again have never learned to be led by the Spirit of God. But those who are regularly led by the Spirit of God become sons of God. They become mature. They grow up. They find God's purpose and destiny in their lives. (We will learn more about being led by the Spirit of God in chapter 8, "The One Who Guides You.")

Do You Want to Know That God Will Provide?

A third aspect of this new life is that the provision for it comes from God. Once you have surrendered yourself to God in obedience to His call, He accepts responsibility for you. I will illustrate this from my experience with the British army, though in many ways the British army is far from being a pattern of God.

I did not enlist in the army; I was conscripted. I entered the army in September 1940 and for the next five and a half years I never had to worry about what I wore, where I would go or what I would eat. My pay in those days (believe it or not) was two English shillings a day! It is hard to fathom how little that was. But we never starved. We did not have to pay for our food, buy our own clothes or secure a place to sleep. For about two years I slept in the North African desert, but at least there was some kind of covering provided for the night. It was no picnic, but the army accepted responsibility for every soldier.

When you commit yourself to God's will without reservation, God becomes responsible to provide for you. There are many people who can testify to this. When I stepped out of the British army and became a full disciple of Jesus Christ, I married a woman who had a children's home just north of Jerusalem. The same day that I married her, I became adoptive father to the eight girls in her home. That is a large family. We went through the war that marked the birth of the State of Israel. In fact, we were right in the middle of it: Our house was about a quarter of a mile from the frontline. After that, we moved from country to country and place to place. We faced dangers, difficulties, opposition—but through it all, God consistently provided for us.

Jesus said in Matthew 6:33, "Seek first the kingdom of God and His righteousness, and all these things shall be added to you." The way of the world is to go about and grab everything in sight. The world makes material possessions—food, clothing, money, houses, cars—its objective. But in this new life, if you make the will of God your objective, God will add these things. That saves a lot of worry if you know that God is the One doing the adding.

Some may say that sounds almost too good to be true. Please realize that it is the promise of Jesus Himself, and He never deceived anyone. There are thousands of servants of the Lord throughout the earth today who will testify from personal experience that it is true. It works. God is as good as His Word.

Let's look at one more beautiful Scripture in the gospel of Mark. Characteristically, it is a brash comment by Peter that brings forth this answer from Jesus.

> Peter began to say to Him, "See, we have left all and followed You." So Jesus answered and said, "Assuredly, I say to you, there is no one who has left house or brothers or sisters or father or mother or wife or children or lands, for My sake and the gospel's, who shall not receive a hundredfold now in this time—houses and brothers and sisters and mothers

and children and lands, with persecutions—and in the age to come, eternal life."

Mark 10:28–30

In this passage Jesus says, "In due course, whatever you have given up will be given back to you, multiplied many times over." Not just in the next world, but in *this* world.

Do You Want to Find Your Tailor-Made Life?

The fourth aspect of the new life is this: If you accept without reservation the call of God on your life, He will see that you are offered the life that He has tailored just for you.

God has made you for a certain life. As we will see in chapter 3, "Seven Steps to Finding Your Place," when you are saved, you are saved to a specific calling. What is more, you will be frustrated and unfulfilled until you enter into that calling. Certainly you can go through life without finding it and end up in heaven, but you will have missed the most important experiences on earth.

From 1940–1949, I was a fellow (member of the governing and teaching body) at King's College, Cambridge. At the end of World War II, the college authorities wrote and offered me a professorship at the university. I wrote back and said, "I've become a Christian. I'm not coming." I could have said it a lot better, but, anyhow, I turned down their offer because God had a different call on my life.

Now suppose I had accepted their offer. At age 65, I would have retired. I would have sat somewhere in a little cottage with a rather moderate pension. But here I am, well past that, traveling the world, strong, active, leading a life that is challenging and exciting.

This life is tailor-made for me. I would be a misfit anywhere else. But in order to find that life, first and foremost, I had to lose the other life. When God called me to the land of Israel and the Jewish people and then to the nations of the world, I actually can say I forsook everything. This was not done in a dramatic way; God just put me in a situation where to obey Him meant that I had to give up all else. I gave up my country, Britain, and settled in a foreign land. I gave up my birth family—not in the sense that I was alienated from them, but their claims came second to the claims of Jesus in my life.

But God is faithful. I would not want to trade my life with anybody—not with the royal family, not with any prime minister, not with anybody. It is the life God appointed for me.

Ponder Your Decision

Do you want to know the job, the place, the relationships, the ministry He has ordained for you? Do you want to enter that special place of provision, responsibility and privilege designed just for you—in this life and into eternity? Are you willing to answer His call?

The Spirit of God is very personal. He may be speaking to you right now, saying to you, *Follow Me. Give your life to Me for My service.* Ponder that for a few moments. Shut yourself in with the Lord. If God has something to say to you, be willing to hear it.

Those early fishermen, Andrew and Peter, were casting their nets into the sea when Jesus walked past and said, "Follow Me." James and John were in the boat with their father when Jesus called them. Scripture records that *immediately* they all left their nets—their means of livelihood—and their family ties, and they followed Him.

You, too, can discover your calling. It is not complicated. In fact, as we will see, it is intensely practical. In this book you will learn to discern your "place" and your giftings. You will grow in the ability to hear the Holy Spirit's voice. You will also discover the greatest obstacle to fulfilling your calling. As you align yourself with the particular calling God has for you, you will face your assignment in these last days with confidence and courage.

Jesus wants to bring you to a place of incredible responsibility and privilege as a king and priest within His Kingdom. (See 1 Peter 2:5, 9; Revelation 1:6.) The powers of hell are working to stop you. What will your decision be? Let's learn what it means to know your calling.

2

What Exactly Is a Calling?

> Therefore, brethren, be even more diligent to make your call
> and election sure.
>
> 2 Peter 1:10

The Scripture above grips me with a sense of its importance. I find that among Christians who know the Lord, very few seem to be making their callings sure. Multitudes of Christians do not even realize what their callings are. I trust I will be able to bring these basic truths of the calling of God home to you in such a way that you will be able to act on them.

The word *call* is the word used in most translations of the Bible. Two alternative words that express the same meaning would be *invitation* or *summons*. The point at which God confronts you with His call is the most significant moment in your life. Your whole destiny for time and eternity will be determined by the way you respond.

In my own experience—having grown up in the Church of England, and having been through its various rituals and ceremonies and requirements—I had reached the age of 24 without ever knowing God personally. In fact, I did not know that it was possible to know God personally.

Then, while serving with the British army, I was suddenly confronted by the call of God through a meeting I attended. I had no doctrinal knowledge of salvation or the new birth or evangelical truth. I was a total stranger to it. But one thing I knew: God had made something available to me and I might never have another opportunity to respond. It was so vivid I knew I had to make a decision, and if I failed to do so, I had no right to expect that He would call twice.

It always grieves me when I see people trespassing on the grace of God—unable to make up their minds and make that commitment. If you have never been confronted by the call of God, and if you are confronted while reading this book, do not assume that you will have a second opportunity. You may. You may have many. But you cannot count on that. In any event, it is discourteous not to respond when God offers you an invitation.

Working Everything Together

The call that God places on each of our lives has direct relationship to His whole purpose and plan. This brings us to the subject of God's supreme sovereignty, a topic we touched on in the last chapter, and our choice to respond to Him or not. Let's begin by looking at this familiar verse:

> And we know that all things work together for good [an alternative translation says that *God works all things together for good*] to those who love God, to those who are the called according to His purpose.
>
> Romans 8:28

Notice the word *called*. God does not work *everything* together for good for *everybody*, but He does for those who have responded to His call. When you respond, you find yourself in a special class around whom all the purposes of God center.

Let me say this to you: If you can grasp this message, you will never again feel like a speck of dust floating in the universe. You will never be an accident looking for somewhere to happen. You will realize that you are an integral part of an eternal plan of God.

Scripture reveals seven phases or actions that God takes to work all things together for good for those who respond to Him. Before the call of God comes in our lives, He has already done these three things: He has *foreknown* us, He has *chosen* us and He has *predestined* us. Only then does He take the fourth action and *call* us. If we respond, He takes the fifth action and *saves* us. This opens the way for God to complete the last two phases: He *justifies* us and He *glorifies* us. Let's look briefly at each of these.

He Foreknew Us

Our calling begins with God's eternal knowledge of each one of us.

> For whom [God] foreknew, He also predestined to be conformed to the image of His Son, that He might be the firstborn among many brethren. Moreover whom He predestined, these He also called.
>
> Romans 8:29–30

The Lord foreknew us. He knew us in advance. He knew us before we were born. He knew us before we were named. He knew us from eternity.

The knowledge of God is truly stupendous. The Bible says, for instance, that He knows all the stars and calls every star by name. Scientists tell us that there are around fifty billion trillion stars in the observable universe. *Billions of trillions* of stars flung through space, and God knows every one of them by name.

God also looks down upon every tiny sparrow. Jesus said that two sparrows are sold for a copper coin, but five sparrows are sold for two copper coins. (See Matthew 10:29; Luke 12:6. Apparently, if you buy sparrows in quantity, you get one sparrow free.) Yet not one of them falls to the ground without God knowing. Somebody once said, "God takes time to attend the sparrow's funeral." There is not one sparrow anywhere in the universe that God does not know about.

Jesus then said, "The very hairs of your head are all numbered" (Matthew 10:30; Luke 12:7). God knows exactly how many hairs you have.

The knowledge of God spans the whole universe from the stars

CALLED *to* CONQUER

The knowledge of God spans the whole universe from the stars to the sparrows to the hairs on your head. It spans not just time, but eternity. If you can begin to sense the totality of God's knowledge, you will have a different attitude about your life.

He Chose Us

Then on the basis of God's knowledge, He chose us. Peter's first epistle describes a certain group of Christians as "elect according to the foreknowledge of God the Father" (1 Peter 1:2). *Elect* is simply another word for *chosen.* These Christians were chosen according to God's foreknowledge.

Your calling is not an afterthought. God does not save you and then say, "Now what am I going to get him to do? What job can I give her in the church?" God saves you because He has a purpose for you.

Can your mind even begin to conceive of that? Before there was a world, before God created anything, He had a plan for you. Do you see how important you are? Nothing grieves me more than to hear Christians talk about themselves as unimportant or insignificant. There is no such thing as an insignificant Christian. Every one of us is vitally important.

Furthermore, when God chooses you to do something for Him, He knows you can do it. He never chooses you to do something that you are not capable of doing by His grace. Never run away from your calling out of fear that you will fail.

He Predestined Us

Then, having known us and chosen us, "He also predestined" us (Romans 8:29).

Some extremists have perverted the meaning of the word *predestined.* God did not predestine us to be saved; He predestined us to be conformed to the image of Jesus Christ. If a person tells me he is predestined to salvation and I see no fruit in his life, I am going to question his statement. But if I see somebody conformed to the image of Jesus Christ, I have to believe it was because he was predestined. It could not happen any other way.

To be predestined means that God has planned the course of your life in advance. He works out the course that your life is to take. He knows where you will be each day of the week, each hour of the day. He knows the problems and the crises that are going to confront you, and He has an answer for every one. God has no emergencies. He is never taken by surprise. Nothing ever happens in the universe that God has not made provision for.

These are the three actions God has already taken concerning us in eternity. God never consulted us concerning any of them. In fact, we knew nothing about them. These three phases did not even happen in time as we know it; they happened in eternity before time began.

He foreknew us, He chose us and He predestined us. Today we marvel at what computers can do. But I tell you, His heavenly computer outdoes all the rest! It is just amazing. There is not a speck of dust in the universe, there is not an insect that God does not know about. And we are part of the central thrust of His plan.

He Calls Us

Continuing with Romans 8:30 we read, "Moreover whom He predestined, these He also called." The fourth phase is the point at which His call comes.

When God has foreknown us, chosen us and predestined us, *then* He intervenes in our lives at a particular moment and *calls* us. The call of God is the point at which God's eternal purposes emerge out of eternity and impact us in time. That is why the call is such a crucial moment in our lives. You may have been like me—living a careless, self-pleasing, materialistic, self-indulgent life, unaware of anything that God had planned for me. Then, in a situation that I certainly would never have planned, I was suddenly confronted by the fact that God had called me, and that my whole destiny was going to be determined by the way I responded. Eternity will be too short for me to praise God for the fact that, by His grace, I said yes.

Believe me when I say that I had no idea what I was committing myself to. God usually does not give us too clear a picture. He did, however, give me, within a few weeks of my calling, a kind of blueprint for my life. God spoke to me through the Holy Spirit and said, *It shall be like a little stream, the stream shall become a river, the river shall become a great river, the great river shall become a sea, and the sea shall become a mighty ocean.* And I thought to myself, *Whatever is God talking about?* But I gradually realized that He was speaking about something that was to be the course of my life.

If you know about the outreach of our ministry today, which probably reaches half the population of the earth, you would have to agree that God's plan has consistently been worked out for more than sixty years and is still being worked out. I used to think I had to do something to make it happen. But the more mature I became, the more I realized it would happen because God said it would happen. All I had to do was stay in harmony with God. Most of the promises that God gives us are far too great to achieve by our own efforts. We just have to embrace them by faith and say, "God, You said it; You'll do it."

He Saves Us

When you respond to the call, He saves you.

I mentioned that I went through 24 years of my life without knowing I could be saved. Maybe you are in that condition, too. I want to tell you, you can be saved and you can know you are saved. Look, first of all, in Thessalonians. Paul is writing to people who had become believers in and disciples of Jesus Christ. He says, "We are bound to give thanks to God always for you, brethren beloved by the Lord, because God from the beginning chose you for salvation" (2 Thessalonians 2:13).

God chose you to be saved. Jesus tells His apostles, "You did not choose Me, but I chose you" (John 15:16). If God had not chosen you to be saved, you never would be saved. The choice is never initially ours; all we can do is respond.

In the work of the Lord, the only choices that have any significance are God's choices. We can vote for a president, we can appoint judges, we can declare someone to be an elder in the church, but if God has not chosen them, there will be no fruit. Jesus says, "I chose you . . . that you should go and bear fruit, and that your fruit should remain" (John 15:16). When we get out of line with God's choice, we can have all sorts of religious effort, but no enduring fruit.

The rest of 2 Thessalonians 2:13 says this: "God from the beginning chose you for salvation through sanctification by the Spirit and belief in the truth." The Holy Spirit prepares you and steers you into the place where you are going to meet the Lord. When you are called of God, you are called to salvation. But the calling of God begins only when you get saved.

I want to make this point very clear: *You may have been saved, but you may have never really discovered your calling*, the purpose for which God saved you. That is a tragedy. I cannot emphasize too strongly the sacredness of the calling of God. It is something of tremendous consequence for every one of us.

He Justifies Us

When He has saved you, there are two final actions in this process: He *justifies* and He *glorifies*.

In Romans 8, the final two phases are put in the past tense: "Whom He called, these He also *justified*; and whom He justified, these He also *glorified*" (Romans 8:30, emphasis added). In God's eternal purposes, those are not new events that will occur sometime in the future. They are eternally established.

This word *justification* is similar to a word we encountered earlier: *predestination*. Like predestination, justification is a rather frightening theological word and people tend to back away from it. But that is a great pity, because justification is really one of the most glorious truths of the New Testament—in fact, of the whole Bible.

What does it mean to be justified? It actually involves a succession of meanings. It means, first of all, to be acquitted of a crime. It is heaven's verdict on your life and mine: "Not guilty." The explanation I have given many times of *justified* is that it means "I'm 'just-as-if-I'd' never sinned." We are reckoned righteous—God imputes righteousness to us. That is because we are made righteous with the righteousness of God, which has never known sin, which has no shadow of guilt, which has no past to be forgiven. We are made righteous with God's righteousness.

25

But we don't stop at just being *reckoned* righteous because we also have to be *made* righteous. Righteousness is received as a gift, but we cannot leave it that way. It requires a response from us. Paul says this very clearly in Philippians 2:12–13: "Work out your salvation with fear and trembling, for it is God who works in you to will and to act according to his good purpose" (NIV).

Justification includes moving from imputed righteousness to outworked righteousness. We do not start with our righteous acts. We start with a righteousness that is imputed to us by God on the basis of our faith for salvation. After that, we work out what God has worked in.

He Glorifies Us

Paul says in Romans 8:30, "Whom [God] justified, these He also glorified." Paul does not conclude his teaching with God saving us. He does not conclude with God justifying us. Paul goes on to the fact that God glorifies us.

Notice again that this verb in Scripture is in the past tense. If you can believe from Scripture that God saved you and justified you, then on the basis of the same Scriptures you can believe that God glorified you. True, there is something wonderful ahead in the future, but being glorified is for us now. It takes place here, in time, in this life.

To be glorified or to enter glorification means that we share Christ's glory with Him. Before Jesus went to the cross, prophetically praying to the Father, He says of His disciples, "The glory which You gave Me I have given them" (John 17:22). Notice that Jesus is not speaking of something that is *going to* happen. It has happened. It was made available through His sacrificial death, His triumphant resurrection and His ascension into heaven.

We are justified through the resurrection of Jesus. But God does not stop with us at resurrection. He takes us beyond resurrection to ascension. Through ascension, we are not just justified; we are glorified. Let me state that again: We are justified through the resurrection of Jesus. We are glorified through the ascension of Jesus.

Paul makes this very clear in Ephesians 2:4–6 (NASB):

> But God, being rich in mercy, because of His great love with which He loved us, even when we were dead in our transgressions, made us alive together with Christ (by grace you have been saved), and raised us up [or resurrected us] with Him, and seated us with Him in the heavenly places in Christ Jesus.

Notice, again, that these three actions God performed are all stated in the past tense: He made us alive together with Christ, He resurrected us with Christ—but don't stop there—He seated us with Him in the heavenly places. On what kind of a seat is Jesus sitting? He is sitting on the throne of God. If we are seated with Him, what are we sitting on? The throne of God. The *New English Bible* actually translates that: "He enthroned us with Him." That translation really brings out the truth. Through His resurrection, we are justified. But through His ascension, we are glorified. We are in glory with Him.

Paul makes this point about glorification in Colossians 3:1–3 (NIV):

> Since, then, you have been raised with Christ, set your hearts on things above, where Christ is seated at the right hand of God. Set your minds on things above, not on earthly things. For you died, and your life is now hidden with Christ in God.

We began this chapter referring to our destiny in God. That is what Paul says in this verse. When Jesus died on the cross, you died along with your whole old, sinful life. Now you are raised with Him; you are enthroned with Him. Your life is hidden with Christ in God. Could you think of a more significant place to be than to have a life that is hidden with Christ in God? Then Paul goes on to say, "When Christ, who is your life, appears, then you also will appear with him in glory" (verse 4, NIV).

Just grasp that fact. Christ is your life. Those four simple words can change the whole way you face life. This is the climax of God's wonderful plan—for us to realize that we are glorified with Christ.

Back to Eternity

In his second letter to Timothy, Paul writes:

> God . . . has saved us and called us with a holy calling, not according to our works, but according to His own purpose and grace which was given to us in Christ Jesus before time began.
>
> 2 Timothy 1:8–9

Notice how again and again Paul looks back to eternity to explain what is happening in our lives. Not one of us can really understand these phases until we view them in the perspective of eternity, because that is where God's plan began. God has called us with a holy calling, not according to our works, but according to His own purpose and grace, which was given to us in Christ Jesus before time began.

If you can grasp what I am saying, you will have a totally different attitude about your life from this point on. If you are experiencing insecurity and uncertainty, I venture to say that it will be dissipated.

You are part of an eternal plan. Furthermore, as one of the elect of God in Jesus Christ, you are the center of the plan. You are not on the periphery. You are not a star somewhere out in some remote galaxy. You are right at the very heart of God's purpose. That is what your calling means. Now let's learn more about how to find your place.

3

Seven Steps to Finding Your Place

The LORD shall preserve your going out
and your coming in.

Psalm 121:8

One aspect of coming to know God's call on each of our lives is wrapped up in a single phrase: *Finding your place.* Until you have found your place, you will never be a totally fulfilled Christian.

Your place touches all parts of your life. God has a geographical place for you, for instance. It matters whether you live in New York or Tokyo or London or Dallas.

The book of Proverbs tells us, "Like a bird that wanders from its nest is a man who wanders from his place" (Proverbs 27:8). Have you ever seen a bird that got out of its nest and could not get back again? Nothing is more weak and pitiful than that bird. That is how it is to be out of your place. I have counseled many people, and sometimes I had to simply tell them, "One of your problems is that you are not in your right geographical place. This isn't the place where you ought to be. And you will never really flourish until you find it."

God's place for you does not stop with geography. He has a place of employment or service for you. He has a specific place for you in

29

the Body of Christ. Scripture says, for instance, that every one of us should be a member of the Body. As such, each one of us must fit into the right place for that member.

My teaching in this chapter is designed specifically to get you into your place. You will not arrive immediately, but if you will act on what you are reading, I believe I can promise you, on the authority of God's Word, that you will get there.

Present Your Body

Paul's letter to the Romans gives us our beginning point for finding our places.

> I beseech you therefore, brethren, by the mercies of God, that you present your bodies a living sacrifice, holy, acceptable to God, which is your reasonable service.
>
> Romans 12:1

You have likely heard the following explanation from me before: When you find a *therefore* in the Bible, you should try to find out what it is *there for*. This chapter begins with a *therefore*: "I beseech you *therefore*, brethren." My answer in this case is that this *therefore* is in Romans 12 because of the previous eleven chapters. Those chapters are the greatest, most perfectly logical and complete unfolding of God's plan of redemption for humanity.

Let me also mention this to you: Never feel the need to be defensive or apologetic for telling some intellectual individual that you believe the Bible. No greater work exists in the field of reasoning and unfolding logic. It is fathomless. You can read it fifty times and every time you will find something in it that causes you to say, "Why didn't I see that before?"

Regarding those first eleven chapters of the book of Romans, I would describe the first eight as the pathway into the Spirit-filled life. Romans 9, 10 and 11 focus on God's dealings with His special chosen people, Israel. This is an essential part of Paul's letter to the Romans, not just an appendix. Why? Because God's plan for the redemption of humanity and the establishment of His Kingdom on earth cannot be fulfilled without Israel.

Everything in the first eleven chapters brings out the fathomless mercy and grace of God, and the total sufficiency of His provision made for us through the death and resurrection of Jesus Christ. It all speaks about what God has done for us.

Then comes the *therefore* of Romans 12:1. How are we to respond? What does God ask from us in return for all He has freely done for us and freely given to us? This really blesses me because the Bible is such a down-to-earth book. God does not ask something super-spiritual of us. He asks something very simple and practical: *Give Me your body. Put your body on My altar as a living sacrifice.* That is the reasonable service—the reasonable response of worship—in view of what God has done. The first step in finding our places is to present our bodies to Him, put them on the altar of His service, and say, "Lord, my body belongs to You."

Paul calls the body "a living sacrifice" because he has in mind the sacrifices of the Old Testament—sheep, goats, bullocks and so on—which were killed and then placed on the Lord's altar. Paul says you must put your bodies on the altar exactly like that ox or sheep or goat. But there is one difference: No one is to kill this sacrifice. God wants a living body.

Once you have placed your body on God's altar in total surrender, your body no longer belongs to you. It belongs to God. You no longer decide what happens to your body. God does. You do not determine what kind of job you are going to do with your body. God does. You do not choose where you are going to live. God does. But it is wonderful when He takes the responsibility.

We all know that when someone owns a piece of property he or she is also responsible for its maintenance. If you live in a rental property, you do not own it and you are not responsible for it. If God just "rents us" (in a manner of speaking), He does not have any responsibility. But if He owns us, He is responsible for the maintenance.

You may never have placed your body on God's altar as a living sacrifice. This is the gateway to knowing God's will and finding your

31

place. You can try avenue after avenue, journey after journey, but if you never complete this step you will never really arrive.

I teach on this topic frequently because it is such an important responsibility. Following is a prayer you can pray if you wish to affirm your decision. This can be a very significant moment, one that affects the rest of your life. Remember, you are praying to the Lord Jesus, the Head of the Church, your Savior.

> *Lord Jesus Christ, I thank You that on the cross You died for me that I might be forgiven, receive eternal life and become a child of God.*
>
> *Lord, I come to You as the Head over the Church. I put my body now, Lord, on the altar of Your service, and I ask You to put me in my place in the Body. I give myself to You without reservation. From this day forward my body belongs to You. It will go where You tell it to go. It will do what You tell it to do. It will say what You tell it to say. It will serve in any way You tell it to serve.*
>
> *Thank You, Lord, for receiving me as I come to You through Your name. Amen.*

Be Renewed in Your Mind

Once we have presented our bodies, we move to the second step:

> Do not be conformed to this world, but be transformed by the renewing of your mind, that you may prove what is that good and acceptable and perfect will of God.
>
> Romans 12:2

When you present your body to the Lord, He does something in you that you cannot do for yourself: He renews your mind. You begin to think differently. You have different motives. Different standards. Different priorities. And because you think differently, inevitably you live differently. You see, God does not transform us from the outside in. He transforms us from the inside out.

Basically religion tries to change people by external practices and rules—what you wear, what you eat, what you drink, where you go, what you can touch, what you cannot touch. Those rules do not change people because it is the inside that matters. God starts from the inside, with your heart, your mind, the way you think and your motives. He says, *When you give Me your body, I will change the way you think. You will be renewed in your mind. You will have different attitudes, different priorities, different reactions. They'll be in line with My will.*

Discover God's Will

With your renewed mind, you will then discover the third step: God's will for your life. You cannot discover God's will in its totality and its perfection until you have presented your body and let God renew your mind.

Look for a moment in the eighth chapter of Romans:

> For those who live according to the flesh set their minds on the things of the flesh, but those who live according to the Spirit, the things of the Spirit. For to be carnally minded is death, but to be spiritually minded is life and peace. Because the carnal mind is enmity against God; for it is not subject to the law of God, nor indeed can be.
>
> verses 5–7

The carnal mind is the way we all think by nature as fallen descendants of Adam. It is our unregenerate way of thinking about ourselves and everything else. That carnal way of thinking is at enmity with God, and God will not reveal His secrets to His enemies. God will not reveal His plan for your life to your carnal mind. But when your mind is renewed by the Holy Spirit through the mercy of God, then you can begin to discover God's will for you.

Romans 12:2 shows us that God's will comes in three phases: *good*, *acceptable* and *perfect*. The further you go in the unfolding of God's will, the better it gets.

The first thing you need to realize is that God's will is *good*. God never wills anything bad for any of His children. The devil will try to persuade you that if you surrender your life to God, you are going to lose an awful lot. Terrible things are going to happen to you. You are going to have to make great sacrifices. You will never enjoy life again. That simply is not true.

I made my surrender to God the night I met Jesus in 1941, and I want to tell you that my life gets fuller and richer and better and more exciting the longer I live. I want to assure you from experience that God's will is good.

Next you find that God's will is *acceptable*. You would not turn it down for ever so much. But you have to embrace it in faith. You cannot say, "God, if You let me do this, then I'll accept Your will." God says, *You accept, then I'll tell you what I'll let you do.*

Then you find that God's will is *perfect*. The final revelation of His will includes every area of your life—every detail, every situation. There is nothing left out. You see, some of what we consider unimportant may be extremely important. If we think God concerns Himself only with important things, we can miss Him.

In 1963 my first wife, Lydia, our adopted African daughter, Jesika, and I immigrated to the United States by accident. I had planned just to come for a visit, but an immigration official told me six months was too long for a visit. So I said, "Help me. What can I do?"

"Well," the official said, "come in, and we'll help you to immigrate." So I immigrated to this great nation by accident. I never intended to become an American citizen (which I accomplished some years later), but it was one of the most important and decisive moves in my whole life. If I had not been led by the Holy Spirit, I would have missed it.

Do you see the distinction? There are some decisions over which I have sweated and prayed and fasted, and they turned out to be unimportant. There are other decisions that have come about casually. I would estimate that I never spent more than an hour buying a house. It has just always been that way. ("This is the house. What is the price? I'll take it.") When my wife Ruth and I went shopping, it seemed we would buy half the store in about half an hour. Neither of us enjoyed shopping, so we would do it once and never think about it again for the next six months. Before we went, Ruth would pray, "Lord, let us be in the right store. Let us be in the right place." We never studied the newspapers to find out where the sales were, but we always ended up with a bargain. That is the leading of the Holy Spirit into God's will.

Be Humble

The fourth step in finding your place comes in verse 3 of Romans 12:

> For I say, through the grace given to me, to everyone who is among you, not to think of himself more highly than he ought to think, but to think soberly, as God has dealt to each one a measure of faith.
>
> Romans 12:3

This is not an easy step for most of us. To put it in my own words: Be humble and realistic about yourself. I want to emphasize that in order to be realistic about yourself you have to be humble, because when you are faced with the facts about yourself, they are humbling. The only obstacle that keeps us from seeing the truth about ourselves is pride. We look in the mirror, for instance, and we say, "Impossible! That's not the way I really look." But it is. So we have to learn to be humble.

Just to be clear, *being* humble is not *feeling* humble. God never says, "Feel humble." He says, "Be humble." Humility is a decision you can make. Jesus gave a good example. He said, "When you are invited to a banquet, My advice is not to sit at the head table because another more important guest will come along and you will be moved down. That will be embarrassing. So when you get to the banquet, sit at the lowest table. There is only one way you can go from there, and that way is up" (see Luke 14:7–11).

John Bunyan put it this way in his book *Pilgrim's Progress*:

> He that is down needs fear no fall,
> He that is low, no pride;
> He that is humble ever shall
> Have God to be his guide.

35

You see, when you are on the floor you cannot go any lower.

Humility always involves a decision—where you will sit or how you will relate to people. Paul says not to think too highly of yourself. The first day you walk into the bank for a job, don't expect to be the president. When you view yourself and your potential ministry, don't start by calling yourself an apostle. Start by being humble, a servant—lowly and teachable. God will see to your promotion. Jesus said, "Whoever exalts himself will be humbled, and he who humbles himself will be exalted" (Luke 14:11). It is your choice.

I was impressed by a poll conducted by a well-known magazine. In answer to the question of who was the most influential person in the world, I believe eleven people were finalists—one of whom was the president of the United States and another of whom was Mother Teresa of Calcutta. As far as I can remember, nearly all of the others selected were in the performing arts. I thought to myself, *What an indication of the generation in which we live, that we cannot distinguish between reality and entertainment!* Most of the people named had nothing to show for their lives. It was all just an act. That is very dangerous.

We must come down to earth and be very realistic. Face the facts. I am overweight. Face the facts. I tell lies. Face the facts. I am envious of other people. Face the facts.

Have you ever discovered that God brings you to the moment of truth before He really helps you? Just when you have given up on yourself, God says, *Now I'm ready to help you. Now you see that you really need My grace. Before that, you thought you could handle it on your own. You can't.* When you are humble and realistic about yourself, you make a wonderful discovery of God's grace and help.

Recognize Your Measure of Faith

The end of Romans 12:3 says this: "Think soberly, as God has dealt to each one a measure of faith." This is next on the unfolding path before you—the fifth step on the journey to your place: You discover that God has given you a specific measure of faith.

There are few things more embarrassing than people who claim to have a lot more faith than they have. It always leads them to disaster sooner or later. The writer of Hebrews says, "Faith is the substance of things hoped for" (Hebrews 11:1). Faith is a substance; either you have it, or you do not have it. Talking about it will not give it to you. You may say, "God, I don't have enough faith." He responds by saying that there are ways you can increase your faith.

I remember a significant time shortly after I was saved when I was serving with the British forces in North Africa. I spent an entire year in a hospital with a condition the doctors were not able to cure. In that condition, I kept saying to myself, *I know that if I had faith God would heal me.* The next thing I always said was, *But I don't have faith.* And when I said that, I was in what John Bunyan calls "the Slough of Despond," the valley of despair.

One day a brilliant ray of light pierced the darkness of the valley. Do you know what it was? "So then faith *comes* by hearing, and hearing by the word of God" (Romans 10:17, emphasis added). If you don't have it, you can get it! It comes. How? By hearing the Word of God. Not by bragging. Not by using super-spiritual talk.

Years ago I called some people forward in a church in Copenhagen, Denmark, for prayer. I was going to anoint them with oil because they were sick. I asked one man, "Do you have faith?"

He replied, "I have all the faith in the world."

My next thought was, *If you have all the faith in the world, what do you mean by being sick?* I knew he would not get healed. I just knew. And, sure enough, nothing happened when we prayed. He had head faith, but no substance. He had the talk, but he did not have the reality.

Jesus said that if you have faith as a grain of mustard seed you can move a mountain (see Matthew 17:20). It is not so much the quantity of your faith that matters, but the quality of your faith. Faith is given to the realistic and to the humble.

Understand That Your Faith Fits Your Place

Why does God give you a specific measure of faith? Here is step six in your development: He has a specific place for you in the Body of

Christ. The faith He has given you is designed for your particular position. If God wants you to be a hand, He will give you hand faith. If He wants you to be an ear, He will give you ear faith. If He wants you to be a toe, He will give you toe faith.

So, you see, if you are a toe and you are trying to be a nose, you are all out of whack. There is a complete imbalance between what you are trying to do and the faith you have. The reason is not because you do not have enough faith. The reason is because you are trying to use your faith for something for which it was not given. It was given for the job and the place you have in the Body.

My hand does a wonderful job as a hand. It opens my Bible, turns the pages—it does everything I ask of it, more or less. But if I tried to do those jobs with my foot, I would be in trouble.

You can almost always conclude that if people are continually struggling for faith, they are trying to do the wrong job. They are a hand trying to be a foot. Or a foot trying to be a hand. This is God's way of guiding you into your place. When your faith fits the place God has for you, then you are not always struggling.

And bear in mind, none of us is sufficient on our own. Every one of us is a member of the Body and we are members of one another. If you are a finger, you must find the hand you should be attached to. You cannot be a finger all alone out in space. If you are a hand, you must be attached to an arm.

One of the big problems with many Christians is the excess of individualism. I have a teaching series on the book of Hebrews, and it includes the twelve "let us" passages. Twelve times the book of Hebrews says, "Let us." It does not say, "Let me." It says, "Let us." It is a corporate decision, a corporate action. There are many things we can never achieve on our own. We must find our place in the Body.

Learn How Your Place Determines Your Gifts

Now we are coming to the last step—and the part that makes most people excited because it involves the gifts. Let's read on in Romans 12:

> For as we have many members in one body, but all the members do not have the same function, so we, being many, are one body in Christ, and individually members of one another. Having then gifts [*charismata*] differing according to the grace that is given to us, let us use them.
>
> Romans 12:4–6

That phrase, *let us use them*, is important. Just to seek for gifts in the abstract, out of context, is foolish and unrealistic. We need to know more specifically what we need.

How do you know what gifts you need? What determines the answer to that question? Your place in the Body. If you are a hand, you need hand gifts. If you are an eye, you need eye gifts. If you are a leg, you need leg gifts. (We will take a closer look at the various gifts available to us in the next two chapters on giftings.)

A good many years ago now, not by my request but rather against my will, the Lord thrust me into the ministry of driving demons out of people. That ministry made me somewhat notorious, unpopular with some and popular with others. Strangely enough, I became unpopular with the people I had always been around and popular with people I never thought would ever love me. That was just one of those anomalies. But when I began moving in this ministry, I discovered gifts God had given me.

I remember a time when a friend of mine brought his sister to Lydia and me and said, "She needs deliverance." I looked at that woman and said, "You need deliverance from—" and I named about eight evil spirits. Then I said to myself, *How did I know that?* Later on, I realized the Lord had given me a word of knowledge. He did not give me that gift out of the blue. He gave it to me when I was in His will and doing the ministry He had called me to do.

So it is with you. You can absolutely trust that God will give you the gifts you need for the job He has called you to do. But do not detach your gifts from your job.

Exercising Your Gifts

So far we have learned that God has a place for you, and on your way to that place, He has been equipping you to function in it.

39

You might not find your way into your final place immediately. It will probably be progressive. But the further you go, the greater the harmony will be between what you are doing and what you have been called to do.

When you have found your place, then you begin to exercise your gifts. I am not suggesting that you are not able to exercise gifts without finding your place, but I can say that the gifts will accomplish God's purpose fully only when you are functioning in your place. Let's look now at the gifts that help us operate in our particular callings.

4

Giftings

The Tools You Need

> Having then gifts [*charismata*] differing according to the grace
> [*charis*] that is given to us, let us use them.
>
> Romans 12:6

God is practical. He would not offer you a place in which you are ill-equipped to function. He would not send you into Kingdom battle without giving you armor and weapons and the training you need to use them. He would not assign you a job without giving you all the tools you need.

The tools are the *charismata*. My friend Bob Mumford says, "Remember, the gifts of the Spirit are tools, not toys." A lot of Christians use them as toys, and that is a misuse. A lot of other Christians want to do the job but do not have the tools. We need to wed the two: the people who want to do the job with the tools they need for the job. In fact, one of the big problems of the Church has been that many Christians are trying to do their jobs faithfully and conscientiously without the right equipment. As a result, they are not able to accomplish what they are called to do. In this chapter and the next I want to help you recognize your particular gifting and enlarge your view of God's call.

The Root of Charisma

Nine different Greek words are all translated by the English word gift. This makes it difficult in some translations of the Bible to understand what it is actually referring to.

We are going to focus primarily on one of the nine words, which is *charisma*. From *charisma* we get the famous word *charismatic*, which is a much misused word. *Charisma* and *charismatic* come from the basic word, *charis*. In the New Testament this is translated as "grace." In secular Greek it is usually translated as "beauty" or "gracefulness." I think the secular translation is illuminating. God sees us as beautiful because we are in Christ.

When I lived in Florida, I was thinking one day about the sun in that beautiful sun-filled state, and this thought came to me: The sun never sees shadows because they are always on the opposite side of the objects it shines upon. That is how I perceive it is with God. He does not see the shadows. He shines the light of His grace upon us, and we shine because of it.

One basic fact about grace that we must understand is that it cannot be earned: Anything that can be earned is not grace. Even so, many people try. They are conscientious. They go to church. They say their prayers. They read their Bibles. But they have never tasted God's grace because they have always felt they had to be good enough.

The problem is, you never can be good enough. That is why, generally speaking, new believers who were profligate sinners understand grace much better and more quickly than religious people. They know they have not earned it and could not possibly earn it, so they just accept it. On the other hand, the "good" people find it hard to stop being good as their means of receiving God's grace.

It depends on your background, to a large extent. If you were brought up in a social system that emphasizes duty, you may find it very hard to know that God just gives gifts freely. The wonderful thing about God's grace is that He is accountable to nobody for it. The book of Job says, "He giveth not account of any of his matters"

(Job 33:13, KJV). God's justice is absolutely exact to the jot and to the tittle, but His grace is free. Oh, how beautiful is the freedom of the grace of God!

Recognizing Your Gifts

Now let's take this a step further. By adding *ma* to the word *charis*, the word *grace,* which is general, becomes specific. So *charisma* is a specific manifestation, operation or impartation of grace. Adding *ta* to the end makes the Greek noun plural: *charismata.* So we see that

> *charis* = grace
>
> *charisma* = a manifestation of grace
>
> *charismata* = multiple manifestations of grace

The purpose of this teaching on gifts is to enlarge your view of your calling and assignment in the Kingdom. It may also help you see that perhaps you already have a *charisma* but you have not recognized it as such. Some of the most important *charismata* are not dramatic. We tend to focus on the dramatic, but, believe me, some of the non-dramatic ones are equally important.

The New Testament gives us a number of *charismata,* which I have placed under four different headings: *Basic, Personal, Spiritual* and *Ministry.* Several of these gifts are mentioned in more than one place in the Bible. In fact, you may want to make your own categories. In this chapter we will discuss gifts from the first three headings and look at the ministry gifts in the next chapter.

Basic Charismata

Righteousness (Romans 5:17)
Eternal life (Romans 6:23)

Personal Charisma

Celibacy (1 Corinthians 7:7)

Spiritual Charismata

GIFTS OF REVELATION:

The word of knowledge (1 Corinthians 12:8)
The word of wisdom (1 Corinthians 12:8)
Discernings of spirits (1 Corinthians 12:10)

GIFTS OF POWER:

Faith (1 Corinthians 12:9)
Workings of miracles (1 Corinthians 12:10, 28)
Gifts of healings (1 Corinthians 12:9, 28)

VOCAL GIFTS:

Kinds of tongues (1 Corinthians 12:10, 28)
Interpretation of tongues (1 Corinthians 12:10, 30)
Prophecy (Romans 12:6)

Ministry Charismata

PERSONS:

Apostles (Ephesians 4:11; 1 Corinthians 12:28)
Prophets (Ephesians 4:11; 1 Corinthians 12:28)
Evangelists (Ephesians 4:11)
Pastors/shepherds (Ephesians 4:11)
Teachers (Ephesians 4:11; Romans 12:7; 1 Corinthians 12:28)

SPECIMENS:

Prophecy (Romans 12:6)
Ministry/serving (Romans 12:7; 1 Peter 4:11)
Teaching (Romans 12:7)
Exhorting/encouraging (Romans 12:8)
Giving/sharing (Romans 12:8)
Leading/ruling (Romans 12:8)
Showing mercy (Romans 12:8)
Helps/assistance (1 Corinthians 12:28)
Administrations/steering (1 Corinthians 12:28)
Hospitality (1 Peter 4:9)
Speaking as God's mouthpiece (1 Peter 4:11)

The Two Basic Gifts

There are two basic gifts, and these are ones that I believe every Christian receives.

Righteousness

You may be surprised to know that the first one is righteousness. In a moment I will tell you why I believe this one comes first. For confirmation of righteousness as a gift, look at Romans 5. This chapter contains a comparison between Adam and Christ. It is done with typical Jewish reasoning, what you could call Talmudic logic. Paul was a Jew of Jews, and here he indulges a little of his Jewish commentary on the Scriptures:

> But the free gift [*charisma*] is not like the offense. For if by the one man's offense many died, much more the grace of God and the gift by the grace of the one Man, Jesus Christ, abounded to many. And the gift is not like that which came through the one who sinned. For the judgment which came from one offense resulted in condemnation, but the free gift [*charisma*] which came from many offenses resulted in justification. For if by the one man's offense death reigned through the one, much more those who receive abundance of grace and of the gift of righteousness will reign in life through the One, Jesus Christ.
>
> Romans 5:15–17

Paul is saying that Adam sinned once and it brought condemnation on the whole race. We have sinned many times but Jesus' one act of righteousness has brought righteousness to all of us.

Righteousness is a gift. If you do not receive it as a gift, you will never get it. Romans 4:3, which is speaking about Abraham, tells us this: "Abraham believed God, and it was accounted to him for righteousness." Abraham did not *achieve* righteousness; it was *imputed* to him. If you want righteousness, you must accept it as a gift imputed to you on the basis of your faith in Jesus Christ. Be grateful for it.

Eternal Life

The next *charisma* that every Christian receives is eternal life. This is found in Romans 6:23: "For the wages of sin is death, but the gift [*charisma*] of God is eternal life in Christ Jesus our Lord."

I believe that, logically, righteousness and eternal life are the first two gifts. You do not qualify for any of the other gifts—in fact, you are not even on the qualifying list—until you have first received the gift of righteousness. On the basis of the gift of righteousness, God gives you eternal life. You see, God cannot give eternal life to people who are not, like Abraham, reckoned righteous.

That is not the end of the process. Your gratitude leads you to respond appropriately, and this is another kind of righteousness. Right at the end of the New Testament, in Revelation 19, we see the Bride of Christ described. She is attired in fine linen, clean and bright, which is the righteous acts of the saints (see verses 7–8). That is not referring to *imputed* righteousness, the gift of God on the basis of faith in Jesus Christ, but to *outworked* righteousness, our actions in response.

In other words, first of all, God imputes righteousness to you. Then you work out what is imputed to you. Paul says in Philippians, "Work out your own salvation . . . for it is God who works in you" (Philippians 2:12–13). What God works in you—you work out. And, by the same token, if you do not work it out, God cannot work any more in. (We will explore this outworked righteousness more fully in chapter 10, "Completing Your Assignment.")

The Personal Gift

Those are the first two charismata, which we might consider basic. The next category of gifting is one I call personal. It is the gift of celibacy. You do not work for it. You do not become ascetic. It is given to you. It is your responsibility only to receive it. I sometimes tell people, "When you ask for a gift, you had better be specific. Otherwise you might get one you weren't thinking of!"

Paul says this: "I wish that all men were even as I myself. But each one has his own gift [*charisma*] from God, one in this manner and another in that" (1 Corinthians 7:7).

What does Paul mean about himself in this context? He means unmarried, celibate. Some of the greatest servants of God have had this gift. Paul was one. Jesus, if you want to say it, was another. Do not have the view that nothing is ever going to happen unless you get married. Abandon that view because if you get married on that basis, your marriage may well be a failure. On the other hand, I am not urging everybody to seek the gift of celibacy.

For myself, I have been married twice, and I am happy being married. But notice, Paul was happy to be unmarried. He said, "I wish everybody were the way I am." Why did God give that gift to Paul? If you study Paul's ministry, you might agree that if he had been married, there could have been only two possible results. Either he would have not been complete in his ministry, or his marriage would have been a disaster. A man who lived like that could not have had a successful marriage.

Personally, I am inclined to think that John Wesley had this gift. He would have been better off if he had never married. The only major mistake he ever made in his life was his marriage, which was a disaster from beginning to end and did nothing for his ministry. We need to be careful that we do not allow ourselves to be dictated to by social standards and customs.

There is another appropriate way of being celibate, which is referred to by Jesus when He says, "There are eunuchs who have made themselves eunuchs for the kingdom of heaven's sake" (Matthew 19:12). Making yourself a eunuch is not the same as receiving a gift. It is a sacrifice, a decision. I believe many wonderful servants of God over the centuries have made that decision.

The Nine Spiritual Gifts

We come now to what I call the spiritual gifts, the nine gifts of the Holy Spirit. Many people think these are the only charismata. These are important, but they are not the only ones.

> But the manifestation of the Spirit is given to each one for the profit of all: for to one is given *the word of wisdom* through the Spirit, to another *the word of knowledge* through the same Spirit, to another *faith* by the same Spirit, to another *gifts of healings* by the same Spirit, to another the *working of miracles*, to another *prophecy*, to another *discerning of spirits*, to another different *kinds of tongues*, to another the *interpretation of tongues*. But one and the same Spirit works all these things, distributing to each one individually as He wills.
>
> 1 Corinthians 12:7–11, emphases added

> God has appointed these in the church . . . *miracles*, . . . *gifts of healings*, . . . *varieties of tongues*.
>
> 1 Corinthians 12:28, emphases added

> Having then gifts differing according to the grace that is given to us, let us use them: if *prophecy*, let us prophesy in proportion to our faith.
>
> Romans 12:6, emphasis added

These gifts have three qualities. One, all of them are manifestations. The Holy Spirit Himself is invisible, but through these gifts He manifests Himself. He impacts our senses in ways that we can see or hear or feel.

Two, all of these gifts are for the profit of all. Through them Christians can minister to one another. They all serve some practical purpose.

Three, all these gifts are supernatural. They are not the product of natural ability or special education. An illiterate person may receive a word of wisdom or a word of knowledge. Similarly, the gift of faith goes beyond the faith that we all need for salvation. It is also distinct from the fruit of faithfulness, which comes by a process of natural growth. This gift speaks of a supernatural faith that goes beyond our natural ability and produces supernatural results.

These nine gifts can be divided into three groups. The first group includes the gifts of revelation. Under this heading are the word of knowledge, the word of wisdom and the distinguishing or discerning of spirits.

The second group includes the gifts of power. Under this heading are faith, miracles and healings.

The third group includes the vocal gifts, gifts that necessarily operate through human vocal organs. Under this heading are tongues, the interpretation of tongues and prophecy.

Some of the gifts are plural in both parts in the original Greek. These include, for instance, gifts of healings, workings of miracles, discernings of spirits, kinds of tongues. This indicates that each healing, each miracle, each discerning, each utterance in a certain tongue (language) is a gift. If a certain gift manifests itself regularly through a certain person, we may say that the person has that gift.

The Word of Knowledge

The first two gifts that Paul lists—the word of knowledge and the word of wisdom—are related in a practical way. A word of knowledge gives us the facts about a situation. Then a word of wisdom tells us what to do about the facts. To put this another way, knowledge is informative and wisdom is directive.

The Word of Wisdom

The purpose of wisdom is to give us right direction. This is brought out in a statement by Solomon in Ecclesiastes 10:10: "If the ax is dull, and one does not sharpen the edge, then he must use more strength; but wisdom brings success" or in the King James Version, "wisdom is profitable to direct." Wisdom directs a person to sharpen the ax, and then the result is success.

In each of these two gifts a word is given, just a little part of God's total wisdom or His total knowledge. God has all wisdom and all knowledge. But praise to His name, He does not dump all His wisdom and all His knowledge out on us because we would collapse under the strain. But when we are in a situation where we need to know something or need direction, and it is not available to us through our natural ability or education or through our senses, then God in His sovereignty gives us a word of wisdom or a word of knowledge.

Discerning of Spirits

I understand the word *discern* to mean the ability to recognize, identify and distinguish between various kinds of spirits that confront us. In this connection we need to bear in mind that the Christian ministry is a ministry in the spiritual realm. In Ephesians 6:12 Paul says we are not fighting enemies of flesh and blood or persons with bodies, but we are arrayed against an evil spiritual kingdom, spirits of wickedness. It is essential that we are equipped to handle our spiritual enemies.

The purposes of this gift, I would suggest, are fourfold. First of all, to lift the veil that covers the unseen spiritual world—the world that we really have to deal with if we are to be effective.

Second, it enables us to see as God sees (see 1 Samuel 16:7). This gift of discerning or distinguishing of spirits enables us to go beneath the outward appearance and see the condition of the heart.

The third purpose of this gift is to protect us from deception. We are reminded that sometimes Satan comes to God's people as an angel of light. He appears to be beautiful and good and wise, but his whole purpose and intention is evil and destructive.

The fourth purpose of this gift is to enable us to diagnose people's problems and so help them—the gift is discerning of spirits, not just discerning of evil spirits. There are various kinds of spirits that engage us in the Christian walk. Let me mention four: first of all, the Spirit of God, the Holy Spirit; second, angels, both good and evil; third, demons or unclean spirits; and fourth, there is the spirit of man, the human spirit.

Scripture gives us some examples of the operation of this gift, including in the ministry of Jesus. The gospel of John, for instance, describes how Nathanael came to Jesus, who declared that here was an Israelite "in whom is no guile!" (see John 1:43–51, kjv).

Probably Jesus was standing preaching and Nathanael was somewhere in the background under the fig tree listening, but Jesus, looking over the heads of those who were closer to Him, saw that face and discerned that guileless spirit. Nathanael was amazed, but Jesus said to him, "This is only the beginning."

Faith

Faith is presented in the New Testament in three different main forms. First is faith to live by. Paul says, "The just [or the righteous] shall live by faith" (Romans 1:17). This faith is an ongoing, personal relationship of commitment to God. It supplies the ability, motivation and direction for the whole Christian life. This is a kind of faith that every Christian has to have to be a Christian.

Next is the fruit of faith, which is listed in Galatians 5. Fruit is always an aspect of character.

The third kind of faith is the gift of faith. This is supernatural faith, a faith above the human level, God's own faith, which is imparted according to the sovereign will of God by the Holy Spirit. In a certain sense the gift of faith is analogous to the word of wisdom and the word of knowledge. It is a supernatural impartation of just a tiny portion of God's own faith to accomplish His purpose in a certain situation.

Working of Miracles

Working of miracles and gifts of healings are closely related; nevertheless, they are distinct. Miracles are frequently instantaneous and visible. The results they produce can usually be seen in some way.

Healings may be gradual and are often invisible. Someone may be healed of a disease like emphysema, for instance, and it may take hours or days or weeks. Healings take place in areas of the body that cannot be seen by the eye.

Gifts of Healings

What is the nature of the healing that is spoken about here? I would say that, in essence, it is God's divine, supernatural power moving through the one who ministers the gift into the body of the one who is sick. Healing is directly related to sickness. Where there is no sickness, there is no need of healing. So, healing is God's power working through a human believer to come against sickness, deal with it and replace it with health.

The gifts of the Spirit are like the colors of the rainbow. They are distinct colors and yet they shade off, one into the other. Healings shade off into miracles, and miracles shade off into healings, and both of them, in turn, are in some way related to faith.

Kinds of Tongues

The gift of tongues is the gift that many people find the most difficult to understand. We need to bear in mind that in the language of the New Testament, the word *tongue* also meant *language*. We can call it the gift of tongues or the gift of languages. We define the interpretation of tongues in that light.

Interpretation of Tongues

Interpretation is the ability, supernaturally given by the Holy Spirit, to present in a known language the meaning of something that has previously been given out in an unknown language. The person who brings the interpretation may be the same person who gave the utterance in the unknown tongue or it may be another person.

Essentially, the purpose of interpretation of tongues as thus defined is the same as that of prophecy. In 1 Corinthians 14:4–5 (NASB), Paul says this:

> One who speaks in a tongue edifies himself; but one who prophesies edifies the church. Now I wish that you all spoke in tongues, but even more that you would prophesy; and greater is one who prophesies than one who speaks in tongues, unless he interprets, so that the church may receive edifying.

The test of the use of these gifts is how much they edify. Speaking in an unknown tongue edifies the one who speaks, but nobody else. But prophesying edifies the church, the assembled company of believers. Prophesying, therefore, is said to be greater than speaking in tongues because it edifies a greater number of people.

When tongues is followed by interpretation, however, then the meaning of the tongue is communicated to the people who can hear and understand, and as a result, it accomplishes the same effect as prophesying would do. So this puts tongues, plus interpretation, essentially on the same level as prophesying.

Prophecy

Prophecy is the ability, granted to a believer by the Holy Spirit, to speak forth words that proceed from God. These words do not come from the believer's own understanding or reasoning or education.

Restoration of the Tools

It is often suggested that these gifts were withdrawn at the close of the apostolic age and are not available today. We read, however, that Paul thanked God for the Christians at Corinth because "you do not lack any spiritual gift as you eagerly wait for our Lord Jesus Christ to be revealed" (1 Corinthians 1:7, NIV). Obviously, Christians are expected to continue to exercise spiritual gifts until the return of Christ. In 1 Corinthians 12:28 Paul says that, among other gifts, miracles and healings have been "set" in the church (KJV). These gifts are part of normal Christian church life.

I believe the key word for God's dealings with His people at this time is the word *restoration*. God is giving back the inheritance we forfeited through unbelief and disobedience. One major aspect of what we are receiving is the restoration of these nine gifts. I have witnessed all nine gifts of the Spirit in operation in places all over the world. These are not theory or doctrine but reality. (For a fuller teaching on the spiritual gifts, please see my book *The Gifts of the Spirit*.)

The fourth category, ministry gifts, is the subject of the next chapter.

5

The Ministry Gifts

Do not neglect the spiritual gift within you.

1 Timothy 4:14, NASB

The word *ministry* is one of those religious words that falls short of conveying its full meaning. On one occasion, I went with a group to Pakistan and the man at the immigration desk said, "What are you?"

I thought for a moment and said, "I'm a minister." He concluded that I was commissioned as a minister in the U.S. government. I got red-carpet treatment from that moment onward. Certainly I was being perfectly honest, but he misunderstood me.

The truth of the matter is that the word *minister* actually means "servant." There are a number of different words in the New Testament for *servant*. One of them is the word from which we get the word *deacon*, which means "a servant." I believe that many churches would be totally transformed if they called their board of deacons "the board of servants." That one title change would transform the attitude of the people, especially the deacons.

The "Person" Gifts

The purposes of these gifts are to build up and mature the Body Christ has constituted in His Church. And the five essential ministries are apostles, prophets, evangelists, pastors and teachers. These ministries have four main functions as defined by Paul. The first is to equip believers to do their work. The second is to build up the Body. The third is to bring us all into unity. The fourth is to produce maturity and completeness. (See Ephesians 4:15–16.)

> And He Himself gave some to be *apostles*, some *prophets*, some *evangelists*, and some *pastors* and *teachers*.
>
> Ephesians 4:11, emphases added

> And God has appointed these in the church: first *apostles*, second *prophets*, third *teachers*.
>
> 1 Corinthians 12:28, emphases added

> Having then gifts . . . let us use them: if *prophecy*, let us prophesy in proportion to our faith; . . . he who *teaches*, in teaching.
>
> Romans 12:6-7, emphasis added

Apostles

Out of these five ministries the first two, the primary ones, are apostles and prophets. The mystery of God's ongoing plan for the Church is revealed through apostles and prophets.

We could think of apostles as the architects or the master builders of the churches. Architects should know all that needs to be known about every stage of the building from the foundation to the roof. They are, by profession and training, responsible for and answerable for every aspect of the project. In the natural realm this is the architect. In the spiritual, it's the apostle. Apostles provide a foundation for a church and are a channel of revelation to a church. (See Ephesians 2:20; 3:4–5.)

The apostle is literally "one sent forth." If you have never been sent forth, you cannot be an apostle. No apostle ever sends himself.

There are a lot of self-appointed individuals going around calling themselves apostles, but they do not fulfill the scriptural requirement. An apostle is sent forth and is answerable to those who send him.

Prophets

In the book of Revelation olive trees appear as a symbol, and they are specifically interpreted as prophets (see Revelation 11). The ministry of the prophet is to be like an olive tree that supplies, continually, the fresh oil of revelation to the lamp stand, which is the Church, so that the lamps on the stand may always burn clear and bright.

A prophet is one who speaks forth. The prophet has a message. It is a message received directly by revelation from God and it is for a specific time, place, situation or group of people. That is what makes him or her different from a preacher who unfolds the general truths of the Word of God. The prophet has a specific message.

Jonah, for instance, was more than a preacher. Jonah could have walked into Nineveh and said, "If you people go on living the way you're living, God is going to judge you." That would have been true. But he had a specific revelation. He said, "Judgment is coming within forty days." That made him a prophet.

Evangelists

The word *evangelist* is derived from a Greek word that means "good news." Evangelists have the specific task to carry the Good News. These are people on the move. They can never stay long anywhere because they are always thinking about the people who have not yet heard the Gospel.

Paul was doing the work of an evangelist in his ministry as an apostle. His apostolic ministry included that of the evangelist. You see, the supreme object of the evangelist is to introduce sinners to the Savior and bring them into salvation and into water baptism. Having made the introduction, he does not stay on to deepen the acquaintance. He goes on to find others who have never yet been introduced.

Pastors/Shepherds

The pastor is the shepherd of the sheep. The Greek word used is *poimen*, and it is regularly translated "shepherd." Only in one place is it translated "pastor" and that is in the list in Ephesians 4:11, but many people do not realize when they read that list that the word is actually *shepherd*.

I have to confess that for years I was, myself, laboring under this confusion in part. I used to speak regularly, for example, about the pastor and elders, as though the pastor was one person and the elders were the others. It was like a flash of lightning, spiritually, when in reading the New Testament one day, I suddenly realized that *pastor* and *elder* are just two different names for the same person or office or ministry. My study of the New Testament Church order was like somebody trying to do a jigsaw puzzle with one extra piece. No matter what I did, there was always one piece that there was no place for. In actual fact this extra piece was, of course, the pastor as a ministry or a person distinct from the elders. *Elder* is one name and *pastor* or *shepherd* is another name for the same ministry.

In Scripture elders were overseers, and their duty was to shepherd the church, which was the flock. Without question, they were the acknowledged leaders of the local church. There was no one above them in the local church. If somewhere in the background there had been a pastor, as we understand it, then Paul's conduct of summoning elders and giving them his instructions would have been extremely unethical. There was no pastor in the background to ignore. These men, collectively, were the pastors or shepherds. They were the elders, the overseers or the bishops.

Teachers

The teacher is the one who unfolds doctrine to the people of God. The person with this ministry gift is essentially an interpreter of Scripture.

As I see it, there are two levels of teaching. There is ministry to the whole Church of Jesus Christ, the Universal Church, and there is ministry specifically to a local congregation.

The teacher who is a minister to the whole Body has essentially a public ministry similar to that possibly of an evangelist or maybe of an apostle. It is mobile and occurs on a fairly large scale. But within the local church there are those who are responsible for teaching on a small scale to individuals and small groups.

This aspect of teaching works in tandem with the evangelists. Paul writes, "I planted, Apollos watered, but God gave the increase" (1 Corinthians 3:6). That simple figure from agriculture gives us a good example. The planting of the seed of the Word of God was the evangelizing. But the seed would never have grown and been fruitful as it should without subsequent watering. And so the next ministry that came along was the watering ministry, and that was the ministry of Apollos, the teacher.

Jesus, the Perfect Example

These ministry gifts are Christ's ascension gifts, the gifts He gave to His Body after He had ascended into heaven. The first step He took was to provide leadership for His people through these gift-ings. That is absolutely basic, because leaderless people are defeated people. Sheep without shepherds invariably scatter. They become prey for wild beasts.

The following point is very important to understand: These gifts are persons. God gave apostles as gifts. He gave prophets as gifts. He gave evangelists as gifts. He gave pastors or shepherds as gifts. And He gave teachers as gifts. Look again at Ephesians 4:7: "To each one of us grace was given according to the measure of Christ's gift." The word *gift* in this verse is different from the word *gift* we have been studying so far. This one is the Greek word *dorea*, and I have a theory about this verse.

This word *dorea* is usually used in the New Testament of a gift that is a divine Person. There are two such gifts. One is Jesus and the other is the Holy Spirit. I suggest from this that these "person" gifts are the gift of a measure of the Person of Jesus.

Let me explain it this way. Jesus is the perfect example of every one of these gifts. He is the perfect apostle, the perfect prophet, the perfect evangelist, the perfect shepherd, the perfect teacher. What a man or woman becomes in his or her ministry is as much as Jesus imparts to that person. So if your ministry resides in one of these categories, it is Christ in you carrying out His ministry as a shepherd, a teacher, an evangelist, a prophet or an apostle.

These ministry gifts are different from the gifts of the Spirit. The gifts of the Spirit are instances in which the Holy Spirit manifests Himself out of the believer. They are brief and temporary. They come and go—like a flash of lightning. But these ministry gifts are life gifts. What qualifies you to be a pastor? It is not the fact that you have been to a seminary. It is the fact that Jesus the Pastor and Shepherd has given Himself back to His people in you. Likewise for an evangelist and the other ministry gifts.

These gifts are totally sovereign; they do not depend on human election. We do not hire a pastor, for instance (God forbid). If you have a hired pastor, you have a hireling. God elects the pastor. All we can do is recognize God's election. The choice is not ours, because the Church is governed from above. The Church is not a democracy; the Head over all things is Jesus, and He operates downward. The first level of His operation is these five main ministries, without which the Church can never function the way it was intended to function.

Our thinking on the wording of these gifts, by the way, has been distorted by tradition and the misuse of words. Many churches will welcome evangelists, for instance, but many of those same churches leave no room for apostles. It is interesting in that regard that just one man in the New Testament was called an evangelist. That was Philip (see Acts 21:8). But I have counted 28 persons called apostles, fourteen before Pentecost and fourteen after Pentecost. As we noted earlier, God has "set" (1 Corinthians 12:28, KJV) these in the church, which leads us to ask: Who has the authority to remove them?

The Specimen Gifts

By specimen I mean gifts that are typical and significant in describing what was operating in the Early Church. In his letters to the Romans and Corinthians, Paul lists nine specimen gifts. Peter, in his first letter, offers two more. These eleven are not an exhaustive list; they are given in Scripture as examples of the work of the Holy Spirit. As you read this, think about each one and ask the Lord, "Which of these charismata do You want me to have?"

Let's return to three Scriptures that note the specimen gifts:

> Having then gifts differing according to the grace that is given to us, let us use them: if *prophecy*, let us prophesy in proportion to our faith; or *ministry*, let us use it in our ministering; he who *teaches*, in teaching; he who *exhorts*, in exhortation; he who *gives*, with liberality; he who *leads*, with diligence; he who *shows mercy*, with cheerfulness.
>
> Romans 12:6–8, emphases added

> God has appointed ... *prophets*, ... *teachers*, ... *helps*, *administrations*.
>
> 1 Corinthians 12:28, emphases added

> *Be hospitable* to one another without grumbling. . . . If anyone speaks, let him *speak as the oracles of God*.
>
> 1 Peter 4:9, 11, emphases added

Prophecy

While a prophet is a "person gift," any individual may be given a prophecy to share. This can be a one-time impartation of the Holy Spirit for a certain situation.

What does a person who prophesies speak to the church? "He . . . speaks edification and exhortation and comfort to men. . . . He who prophesies edifies the church" (1 Corinthians 14:3–4). Prophecy is limited to edification, exhortation and comfort because God does not discourage and beat down believers. He does not pour forth warnings of judgment against believers, but unbelievers.

The word *edification* may seem a little old-fashioned and ecclesiastical-sounding. Most people are familiar with the term *edifice*, which is a building. *To edify* simply means "to build up or strengthen." It means to make people more effective as members of the Body of Christ in whatever particular ministries they have. If you receive the gift of prophesying, then, it should make you better able to serve the Lord and His people.

Exhortation means "to stimulate, to encourage, to admonish and to stir up." Admonishment can include severe warning and even rebuke; however, exhortation does not include condemnation. "There is therefore now no condemnation to those who are in Christ Jesus, who do not walk according to the flesh, but according to the Spirit" (Romans 8:1).

Comfort, in contemporary words, means "to cheer up."

I mentioned above that true prophecy, and exhortation in particular, do not bring condemnation. I want to emphasize this point again because, over the years, I have heard many instances of people claiming to prophesy, yet the total effect could be summed up as confusion and condemnation. That is not a genuine manifestation of the Holy Spirit. God is never the author of confusion, nor does the Holy Spirit ever minister condemnation to the people of God.

True prophesying does not serve the devil's purpose; it *undoes* the devil's purpose. If so-called prophesying condemns and discourages, it is doing the devil's work. Two of Satan's greatest and most frequently used weapons against God's people are condemnation and discouragement. If an influence, suggestion or message comes into your life that has the effect of discouraging you, do not attribute it to the Holy Spirit.

One of the problems is that many Christians believe they are being humble when they feel condemned and subsequently go around telling people how bad they are. Yet if you are a new creation in Jesus Christ and are God's handiwork, then every time you criticize yourself you are criticizing God's work. You are not glorifying God; you are glorifying the devil.

Ministry/Serving

The Greek word for *ministry* means "serving." It is related to the word from which *deacon* is derived. This is essentially a form of service in the material realm of life.

Serving is the pathway in the Body of Christ to leadership. I don't think the Lord ever takes somebody and immediately makes him a leader. Jesus called His disciples to Him and said this: "Whoever desires to become great among you, let him be your servant. And whoever desires to be first among you, let him be your slave" (Matthew 20:26–27).

You will notice that the higher up you want to go, the lower down you have to start. If you are going to be simply "great," you have to become a servant. But if you are going to be "first," you have to become a slave.

Teaching

Teaching, like prophecy, is a repetition of one of the person gifts we looked at earlier.

The goal of our instruction is love. I have come to believe that any instruction that does not produce love is missing the goal. The first Scripture we are turning to, however, could possibly moderate your enthusiasm for seeking this wonderful ministry gift. It is this: "My brethren, let not many of you become teachers, knowing that we shall receive a stricter judgment" (James 3:1).

I have pondered the full meaning of that and understand a teacher in that connection to be a teacher of doctrine. Acts 2:42 says this about the new believers in Jerusalem: "They continued steadfastly in the apostles' doctrine and fellowship, in the breaking of bread, and in prayers." The primary requirement of teaching is to continue in the apostles' doctrine. Wherever churches have departed from the apostles' doctrine they have ended up in trouble and in failure. I believe that the ministry that James was talking about was this teaching of biblical doctrine.

There are two levels of teaching. There are those who initiate and those who reproduce. Those who initiate have the responsibility to determine what to teach. Those who reproduce teach what they have been taught.

In 2 Timothy 2:2 Paul says: "The things that you have heard from me among many witnesses, commit these to faithful men who will be able to teach others also." I have heard it pointed out that four generations are represented in that verse. There is Paul, there is Timothy, there are the faithful men that Timothy teaches and there are the faithful men that they will teach. They were to teach what Paul had taught Timothy. This is, in a sense, remaining in the apostles' doctrine.

Exhorting/Encouraging

I have listed this ministry gift as *exhorting* or *encouraging* because the Greek word that is used is the word for "encouraging." Would you agree that the Body of Christ tremendously needs the ministry of encouraging? I think discouragement is one of the devil's strongest weapons.

The word used here has two meanings, and we can say them rather well in English: to "cheer up" or to "stir up." If people are discouraged, you cheer them up. If people are lazy or weary, you stir them up.

Giving/Sharing

The Greek word for *giving* literally means "sharing." You may not have realized that sharing is a ministry. This is one reason why I do not believe that God wants all Christians to be poor. God blesses some Christians with wealth. Why? Because He has given them a ministry of sharing. They use their wealth for the Kingdom of God—to bless other servants of God, to help the work of a ministry.

What I am about to say may seem indiscreet, but I want to tell you that as I pray for the Kingdom of God these days, I am praying that God will redirect the finances in His Kingdom to the persons, ministries and operations that are doing what He wants done. I see an awful lot of money going down the religious drain, so to speak, and it grieves me. Giving, or sharing, requires a great deal of wisdom and sensitivity to the Holy Spirit.

Leading/Ruling

In the *New American Standard Bible* and the *New International Version*, the word *lead* is translated "rule." It means "to stand out in front."

Paul teaches that if a man cannot manage his own family, he cannot manage the church of God (see 1 Timothy 3:5). It is the same word used here. It means to take responsibility for, to be a leader, to be "out in front," to be a protector. It means to stand between the people you lead and the forces that oppose them. Without leadership, any operation founders.

Showing Mercy

"[Show] mercy, with cheerfulness" (Romans 12:8). How desperately we need this ministry! When I was sick that year in a hospital in Egypt, a dear woman of 75, a Salvation Army brigadier, undertook a difficult journey all the way from Cairo to Alballah to visit me. That visit transformed my life. It initiated something totally new in me, which has gone on to this day. How I thank God for that lady who would make a sacrifice like that to visit an unknown British soldier in a hospital!

That was the ministry of showing mercy. From that time onward, everything in my ministry has to be credited partly to that dear woman. She passed on to glory many years ago, but I always think of what is still being laid up to her account in heaven by the mercy she showed me.

Helps/Assistance

For the next two *charismata* we return to 1 Corinthians 12:28, where the person gifts are also given:

> And God has appointed these in the church: first apostles, second prophets, third teachers, after that miracles, then gifts of healings, helps, administrations, varieties of tongues.

Miracles, healings and tongues, of course, are included in the list of the nine spiritual gifts of the Holy Spirit (see 1 Corinthians 12:7–10). But we find two other gifts in verse 28 that qualify as ministry gifts. The first is *helps*, the second is *administrations*.

The meaning of *helps* should be fairly obvious. They say in America that there are chiefs and there are Indians. Being a help is being an Indian.

There was a time in the Pentecostal movement in Britain (when I was living there way back in the 1950s) when everyone wanted to be a chief. Nobody wanted to be "helps." And nothing got done! It all fell apart. Maybe God has chosen you to be a helper.

Administrations

Administration is an interesting word. It is taken directly from the Greek word for "to steer." It does not mean ruling; it means the act of steering, of turning the rudder. This is a ministry that, by making just one little move, changes the course of a group, the course of a meeting or whatever it may be.

This is a very fascinating *charisma* to observe. Many, many times in a meeting, for instance, at a certain point God wants us to go one way and we have our minds made up to go another. We have decided we are going to sing choruses tonight. God does not want us to sing choruses; God wants us to do something different. Or we plan on having a Bible study tonight, but God calls us to prayer. The ministry of steering is just indicating the way the group should go and turning the rudder so that it goes that way.

Hospitality

In 1 Peter we find two interesting *charismata*:

> *Be hospitable* to one another without grumbling. As each one has received a gift [*charisma*], minister it to one another, as good stewards of the manifold grace of God. If anyone *speaks*, let him speak as the oracles of God.
>
> 1 Peter 4:9–11, emphases added

The first gift listed in this reference is in verse 9: "Be hospitable to one another." How many of us recognize that hospitality, taking care of the needs of others, is a *charisma*? (And, by the way, how many of us are aware that grumbling is a sin?)

A Jewish proverb says, "One hand washes the other and both hands wash the face." That is how it should be. The whole body is interdependent.

Speaking as the Mouthpiece of God

Finally, the last gift is speaking "as the oracles [or mouthpiece] of God" (verse 11). Some people have the last word—right in the middle of a conversation. After that, nothing more needs to be said. This is not to say that every word that person speaks is an oracle of God, but in certain cases he or she speaks with a certain kind of authority that is not debated.

My first wife, Lydia, was like that. She would come out with a sentence of about ten words, and after she had said it, there was nothing more to say. Sometimes they were sharp sentences, too!

Think It Over

Please take some time and think over these four lists of gifts: basic, personal, spiritual and ministry. As we pray for God to show us our places, we should also ask that He indicate the charismata that we need and that He wants to give us. Here is a pattern prayer you may wish to use:

> *Father, I thank You for Your Word, which is so clear, so specific and so practical. As I have looked into Your Word, I have begun to see the relationship between my place in the Body and Your charismatic gifts. Lord, I pray that from this moment onward You will guide me into my rightful place in the Body—and in every other way as well. Help me to exercise the faith You have given me to bring into action the particular charismatic gifts that are appropriate to my place and function. I commit myself to You, Lord. In Jesus' name, Amen.*

A beautiful Scripture in Ephesians speaks of those of us who have received Jesus as Savior:

> For by grace you have been saved through faith, and that not of yourselves; it is the gift of God, not of works, lest anyone should boast. For we are His workmanship, created in Christ Jesus for good works, which God prepared beforehand that we should walk in them.

Ephesians 2:8–10   67

Never underestimate yourself or your giftings, because you are God's workmanship. Remember: If you speak negatively about yourself or your giftings, you are criticizing the work of His hands. The Greek word used here for *workmanship* is *poiema*, which gives us the English word *poem*. It suggests a creative masterpiece. When God wanted to show the whole universe what He could create, He decided on us. Is that not remarkable?

You are God's creative masterpiece, created for a purpose. For what purpose? For good works, which God has prepared beforehand for you to walk in. That is your calling, your assignment. When God created you in Christ, He had something for you to do. You never have to sit down and ponder, "What am I to do?" You need to ask: "God, what do You have for me to do?" There is not a single person on earth today created in Christ Jesus for whom God does not have a specific calling.

One person who knew that principle very well was Lydia. Her story is told, in part, in the book, *Appointment in Jerusalem* (Chosen, 1975). The key Scripture in her experience was Ephesians 2:10: "For we are His workmanship, created in Christ Jesus for good works, which God prepared beforehand that we should walk in them." She was in a hotel in Stockholm one day looking down on the people in the street milling to and fro, and she said to herself, *Does it really make any difference where they go or where they come from?* God impressed that verse upon her, and she realized that God had created her for a special task that no other person could do.

Once she realized that, she said, "God, if You have a special task for me that no other woman can do, I'm ready to do it." God gave her a most unusual assignment. She had to give up her position in Denmark as a teacher and go to Jerusalem without any missionary organization or any church to support her. Then she was directed to take in one little dying Jewish baby, and thus began a children's home that lasted for twenty years. Lydia had a special task. We all have a special task. The principle applies to every one of us.

Do you know what the good works are for which God created you? You may not know them all, but are you beginning to have some direction? As you continue to discern and grow and listen, you will find, like countless others, that you must learn to lay everything else aside that would hinder you from finding your assignment in the Kingdom.

You also will soon discover that the enemy has not been idle during your exploration. He intends to defeat you from finding the joy and fulfillment of your calling. In the next two chapters, we will observe his strategy, how it manifests and what our response should be.

6

The Greatest Obstacle
to Fulfilling Your Call

They have rejected the law of the LORD of hosts and despised
the word of the Holy One of Israel.

Isaiah 5:24, NASB

In this chapter I want to present what I consider to be the greatest
single hindrance to fulfilling one's calling at the present time. I
think that this force especially targets men—and even more particularly men who would be leaders in the church. If I were to give
you a hundred guesses, I do not believe you would guess correctly.

The particular force that hinders Christian men and women from
fulfilling their callings and achieving their destiny in God is *witchcraft*. It is the major enemy of God that binds millions of individuals
from fulfilling their calls and being effective in God's army. I believe
that witchcraft is a worldwide phenomenon; it has the capacity to
adapt to the particular cultural context in which it is operating.

Paul gives us interesting insight about this power at work in the
Church. The text we will begin with is found in Galatians 3:

> O foolish Galatians! Who has bewitched you that you should not obey the truth, before whose eyes Jesus Christ was clearly portrayed among you as crucified?
>
> Galatians 3:1

In 1963 I took over the pastorate of a church in a city on the West Coast of the United States. I was told that the board of the church had unanimously invited me. Being unwary in those days and not familiar with American church life, I stepped into the devil's trap. There were twelve members on the board and when I arrived I discovered they were the only twelve people in the church! Within a month all the members of the board had stepped down from their positions. I found myself in a difficult and precarious situation. What really baffled me was the attitude of this small congregation. Though they were Pentecostal, they were like people who were beaten down and incapable of being happy or free.

I had never dealt with a situation like that in my life and I turned to God in desperation. He gave me Galatians 3:1. He said, *They are bewitched*, and I had to believe it. There was no other adequate explanation for the condition of those people.

I discovered quickly how they had been bewitched. The wife of the previous pastor was a gifted but dominating woman. In the course of the previous two or three years she had divorced her husband (the pastor), the leading board member had divorced his wife, and the pastor's wife and the board member had then married. If you can get away with that type of behavior in a Pentecostal church, there has to be some unusual explanation. She had so subdued those people they would not dare to resist anything she said or did. It was a most amazing situation.

When I realized I was dealing with witchcraft, I began to seek God for scriptural answers and scriptural weapons. Ultimately, Lydia and I prevailed in that situation. We defeated witchcraft in the church and we saw God's blessing return.

But that was a vivid personal lesson. Never before that experience had I ever conceived that Christians could be bewitched. And yet there it was right in Galatians 3:1: "Who has bewitched you?" If you read the verses that follow after, you will discover that those people were saved and baptized in the Holy Spirit. They had witnessed God's miracles, and yet they had become bewitched. If it could happen to the Galatians, why should we assume that there is a Christian to whom it could not happen?

The Nature of Witchcraft

I want to tell you a little bit about the nature of witchcraft—first of all, in general, and then in the Church.

There are three related words in English—*witchcraft*, *divination* and *sorcery*. One translation of the Bible will use the word *witchcraft*, another may use *divination* or *sorcery*. Essentially they are three layers of one and the same cake—with a certain difference.

Witchcraft is the dominating force. It operates outside the Church, in the natural, by curses and spells. And let me tell you, curses and spells are very real.

Divination is essentially the fortune-telling aspect. It seeks to disclose the future. If you go and have your palm read or go to a fortune-teller, you are going to a diviner, to someone who practices divination. Let us remember that had we lived in Israel under the Law of Moses, the penalty for that trip to the diviner was death!

Sorcery operates through objects such as charms or talismans or drugs. The whole drug culture is an aspect of sorcery. Sorcery also operates through music. A great deal of rock music today is simply an operation of sorcery—it bewitches people. Watch the eyes of young people after they have been listening to that kind of music. They are glazed. They are out of touch with reality. There is a satanic power behind that music that captivates them.

This is not new in the world. You only have to go to Africa, for instance, and have any interaction with a witch doctor there. You will find all those aspects—the curses, the spells, the fortune-telling, the use of charms or music to captivate people. Much of the drum music we have today among our young people comes from Africa. It went by one roundabout route—by way of South America to North America. From North America it has basically spread around the world.

The Connection with Rebellion

I am going to use the term witchcraft from here on, but understand that it covers the whole spectrum: witchcraft, divination and sorcery.

Witchcraft is closely connected with rebellion: "For rebellion is as the sin of witchcraft" (1 Samuel 15:23). Wherever you find rebellion, you will end up with witchcraft. Those words were spoken by the prophet Samuel to King Saul because he had deliberately disobeyed God's word. Samuel rebuked the king and said, "Your rebellion against the word of God is just the same as witchcraft." It is no accident that before King Saul died he was consulting a witch. That is cause and effect.

In America, as one example, the generation of young people in the 1960s was largely a drug culture, and that lifestyle was basically one of rebellion. They were rebels against parents, rebels against the government, rebels against institutions, rebels against the Church and so on. And almost without exception they ended up in the occult.

The relationship between rebellion and witchcraft is important to understand. Rebellion sets up illegitimate rulership; that is, rulership that is not of God. Witchcraft is the power that supports the illegitimate rulership. So wherever there is illegitimate rulership you will find that it will normally operate through witchcraft.

In Galatians 5:20 Paul lists witchcraft as one of the works of the flesh, so it is an aspect of the nature of fallen man. Man was created by God to rule—but he was created to rule under God's authority. When he rebelled against God's authority, he lost the right to rule, but he never lost the desire. Once he fell, he was prone to use illegitimate power in order to rule.

So, what is initially simply an aspect of the fallen nature—the desire to manipulate people and get them to do what you want—exposes such people to the spiritual force of witchcraft and then they are no longer free agents. They are no longer doing it because it is their character to do it; they are doing it because they are controlled by a spirit that makes them do it.

And so we get to the spiritual situation spoken about in Galatians 3:1, where an evil force was at work in the church in Galatia. This was not just fallen human nature—although the door by which it entered was fallen human nature—but it was a dark, evil, satanic power that was frustrating all the purposes of God for that church.

The key words when you think of witchcraft are *control, domination, manipulation* and *intimidation*. Wherever you run into those operations—people who control others, who dominate others, who manipulate others, who intimidate others—you have run into Satan. God does not utilize those practices. God allows liberty in human individualism; witchcraft suppresses it. Witchcraft prefers to dominate, but if it cannot dominate, it will manipulate. It occurs in all sorts of settings. Here are three examples from ordinary life.

Husband and Wife

God has ordained that a wife should be under the authority of her husband. I fully recognize, of course, that this can be sadly abused by the husband, and in this day of rampant divorce and male abdication, many women have been forced to head the home in order to rear the children and pay the bills when husbands are absent. But where a wife purposely takes over the leadership role in a family you will find witchcraft, because she will usually do it by manipulation.

There are countless ways for a wife to manipulate. Every time her husband says or does something she does not like, she can throw an emotional fit. That will wear her husband's nerves down. So to avoid the emotional fit, he bypasses the issue and his wife gets her way.

I once encountered a situation of a dear Christian woman who was married to a minister. They had a family of five children, and were really committed Christians. But she had an occult background before she became a Christian and she was not altogether free from that influence. Without realizing it, she dominated her family.

One of the ways that it manifested was that if something happened in the family that she did not like, she got the most intense migraine imaginable. Then the whole family had to tiptoe around because "Mother's got a migraine." To avoid the agonies of Mother's migraine everybody gave in to her. That is manipulation. Most of the time manipulation is not a conscious decision. It is done because there is something in the person that causes him or her to do it.

Parents and Children

God has given parents authority over their children, but many times it is the children who run the parents, and they do it by manipulation. For instance, little Johnny does not get his way so he throws a temper tantrum—especially in front of guests. His mother and father are so embarrassed that in order to hush him up they give Johnny what he wants. What is that? Manipulation.

Parents, if your children throw temper tantrums more than two or three times, it is possible that a demonic spirit may enter into them in those tantrums. After that, you will not be manipulated by your child, but by the spirit in your child—and even a very small child may have a very strong spirit. Never judge the force of the opposition by the size or the age of the child. It is not the child but the spirit in the child that is in control.

I tremble when I see parents allowing their children to display their temper fits. A brother in the Lord from India acknowledged that this is common among Asian children. Most of those children have demons in them, which enter when the child is not restrained.

Parental discipline is designed to protect children from spiritual forces that are too strong for them to hold out against by themselves. If parents do not exercise discipline, the children are exposed to these spiritual forces.

Pastor and Congregation

A common occurrence in churches is the woman "prophetess" who runs the church by her prophecies. You would be surprised how many pastors in small Pentecostal churches are dominated by one or two women. These two women are the only ones who ever get interpretation of tongues, and basically their interpretations tell the pastor what to do. And woe to that unhappy young man if he ever parts company with his prophetesses.

There are many, many other examples, but these show that illegitimate rule is supported by an illegitimate spiritual power, which is witchcraft.

How Witchcraft Defeats the Church

The Bible mentions two main types of witches—male and female. The word witch happens to be feminine. The masculine form is *wizard*. Because the word witch is more familiar in religious circles, we tend to think of witchcraft as something exclusively female, but that is an unjust position to take because the first real aggressive witch (or wizard) in the Bible was a man. His name was Balaam.

Balaam was a fortune-teller, a soothsayer and a witch doctor. He was hired by Balak, the king of Moab, to curse Israel. Balak said to him, "I know the ones you curse are cursed, and the ones you bless are blessed." (See Numbers 22–24 for the whole story.) Many people in Africa say something similar to the witch doctor: "If you bless my family, I'll be blessed; and if you curse my enemy, he'll be cursed." That is essentially the province in which this type of witchcraft operates.

The female type of witchcraft is found in the example of Jezebel, the wife of King Ahab, who manipulated her husband and ran the kingdom through him. One of the most characteristic actions that she performed was to take the signet ring of authority from her husband and sign the death order for Naboth whose vineyard they wanted to take. (See 1 Kings 21.) That is witchcraft. It is taking the male authority symbol and using it to promote the female's purpose.

Both of these two types of witchcraft from the Old Testament, male and female, are mentioned in the New Testament in the context of the Church. Not outside the Church, but in the Church. Balaam is mentioned in 2 Peter 2:15 in connection with false prophets. Balaam is also named in the same context in Jude 11, and he is listed as one of the evil influences found in one of the seven churches of

Revelation (see Revelation 2:14). Jezebel is referred to in Revelation 2:20 in connection with another of the churches:

> Nevertheless I have a few things against you, because you allow that woman Jezebel, who calls herself a prophetess, to teach and seduce My servants to commit sexual immorality and eat things sacrificed to idols.

I note that because I want you to see that though these types of witchcraft are outside the people of God, their greatest aim is to insinuate themselves inside the people of God.

As we observe the workings of these two types of witchcraft, we soon understand these two tactics it uses: If witchcraft cannot defeat us directly, it will seek to destroy us from the inside. Look at the example of Balaam. First of all, witchcraft seeks to curse God's people directly. Balaam was hired to curse Israel, but as long as Israel was in obedience to God, God would not permit Balaam to curse them. Every time Balaam tried to curse Israel he ended up by blessing them—much against his own will and much to the chagrin of King Balak who had hired him.

If you read the Bible carefully and you have to put together several different passages, you will find that Balaam did not give up. This is typical. Knowing that he could not curse Israel directly, he tried the second approach. He recommended that King Balak entice Israel into welcoming the Moabite women into their midst and worshiping their idols. When the king had succeeded in bringing this sin into their midst, the curse came upon Israel from God, not from Balaam.

This is how witchcraft works. If it cannot defeat us directly it will seek to entice us into something that causes God's curse to come upon us because of the way God has ordered the universe.

The Fifth Column

You see, the Church is never defeated from without. Jesus said about His own experience, "The prince of this world, the devil, is coming and he has nothing in Me" (see John 14:30).

Because the devil had nothing in Him, the devil could never defeat Him. If the Church could say, "The devil has nothing in us," the Church would be invincible. The devil defeats the Church through the fifth column.

Let me tell you the origin of the phrase *fifth column*. It so happened that I was on a walking tour in 1936 with a friend of mine. I was 21 years old and we were going over the Pyrenees from France to Spain. We found ourselves in Spain in the middle of a civil war, which we had not anticipated. In this civil war, two different factions of Spaniards were fighting one another, and General Franco was the one who ultimately emerged victorious.

This story is related about a certain Spanish general who was attacking a Spanish city. Another general came to him and said, "Tell me, general, what is your plan to capture this city?"

So the first general said, "Well, I have four columns advancing on the city—one from the north, one from the south, one from the east and one from the west." Then he paused and added, "But it's my fifth column I'm expecting to take the city for me."

So the second general asked, "And where is your fifth column?"

The first general replied, "Inside the city."

The fifth column is the group of traitors inside who betray the city to the attackers from without. It is only the fifth column in the Church that ever permits us to be defeated. We are never defeated from without, whether it is individually or corporately.

If I can say, "The devil has nothing in me," then the devil cannot defeat me in any way. If we could say as a group of Christians, "The devil has nothing in us," the devil would be powerless against us. That is why Satan's most persistent strategy is to insinuate himself, his agents and his forces into the midst of the Christian Church.

In the next chapter we will turn from the general to the particular, and observe the effect of witchcraft on the Church.

7

The Enemy in the Church

Woe to those . . . who substitute darkness for light.

Isaiah 5:20, NASB

When Paul confronted the Galatians with the revelation that they were being bewitched, he began with these three words: "O foolish Galatians!" None of us likes to be called foolish! But we have to admit that there are many foolish Christians.

Paul did not mince words, and, as we saw in the last chapter, revealed their folly: "O foolish Galatians! Who has bewitched you?" The Greek word for *bewitched* means literally "to smite with the eye." This is referring to the "evil eye." A Greek Orthodox priest came to me some years back who was baptized in the Holy Spirit. He came to me for help because somebody had "put the evil eye on him," and he used the same word that is used in Galatians, *baskaino*—in essence, someone actively and deliberately placed a curse upon him. Mark 7:21–23 says:

> For from within, out of the heart of men, proceed evil thoughts, adulteries, fornications, murders, thefts, covetousness, wickedness, deceit, lewdness, an evil eye, blasphemy, pride,

foolishness. All these evil things come from within and defile a man.

This priest was very well aware that this evil eye is real. Let's look further at the Galatians text:

> O foolish Galatians! Who has bewitched you that you should not obey the truth, before whose eyes Jesus Christ was clearly portrayed among you as crucified? This only I want to learn from you: Did you receive the Spirit by the works of the law, or by the hearing of faith? Are you so foolish? Having begun in the Spirit, are you now being made perfect by the flesh?
>
> Galatians 3:1–3

Whatever results the Galatians produced were produced by witchcraft.

The Expression of Witchcraft

What name would we give to the problem of the Galatians in modern theological language? The word is legalism. When I realized that legalism is the expression of witchcraft in the Church, it really shook me, because I saw the whole nature and operation of the Church in a completely different light.

Does it seem unlikely to you that legalism is perhaps the number one problem of Christians? Does it seem even less likely that this problem is an aspect of witchcraft? You may say, "It couldn't be, Brother Prince." But then we have to ask ourselves: Are we so much better than the Galatians? They were a real live New Testament church, filled with the Spirit and witnessing miracles. They had the apostle Paul preaching to them *in person*. How many contemporary churches can claim that they are far superior to the Galatians?

Legalism is usually a derogatory term we use to describe people who disagree with us. Let me offer two possible definitions of legalism. First of all, legalism is "seeking to achieve righteousness by keeping rules or law."

Most translations of the New Testament state that righteousness does not come by observing the law. Note that the word *the* has been put in by translators. What the text actually says is *righteousness does not come by observing law.*

The pattern of law is the Law of Moses, but it is not confined to the Law of Moses. In other words, the Law of Moses is the pattern law because it was a divine law, a perfect law. It was a God-given law. If righteousness cannot be achieved by observing the Law of Moses, then there is no other law that can possibly produce righteousness.

The second possible definition of *legalism* is "adding to God's requirements for righteousness." This is demanding people to do more than God demands of them, which is really putting oneself in the place of God. If God says this is all you have to do, then no church or minister or religious body has any authority to add one more requirement.

The Internal Seduction of Witchcraft

To understand how witchcraft operates, let's look again at what Paul says in verse 1: "Who has bewitched you that you should not obey the truth, before whose eyes Jesus Christ was clearly portrayed among you as crucified?" (Galatians 3:1).

These words imply that witchcraft operates by blinding the people of God to what was achieved by the death of Jesus on the cross. Being blinded, they then have to turn to other sources of righteousness.

There are three aspects of what Jesus accomplished on the cross that are pertinent here, all of which are relevant to law. First, He abolished law as a means of achieving righteousness with God, once and for all: "For Christ is the end of the law for righteousness to everyone who believes" (Romans 10:4). Catholic or Protestant, Jew or Gentile, it is the same for everybody. Once you become a believer, you are shut off from law as a means of achieving righteousness with God.

Second, and this is not appreciated by most people, what Jesus experienced on the cross is the demonstration of God's judgment on our fallen, carnal nature. Romans 6:6 says, "Our old man [our carnal nature] was crucified with Him." The mercy of God is that instead of doing it to us, He did it to Jesus. But if you want to know what God thinks about our unregenerate, carnal nature, picture Jesus on the cross—because that is God's last word about it. The cross was made for our carnal nature and the cross is where it belongs. We will discuss this topic of the fallen nature of man in more depth in chapters 9 and 10.

Third, there is a message in the cross that applies to the way we live. The cross is not merely something external where our redemption was purchased; it is also an inner principle that has to apply to our lives. Paul says in Galatians 5:24, "Those who are Christ's have crucified the flesh with its passions [affections] and desires [lusts]." We could not do this if God had not done it in Jesus. The principle of the crucified life—the denial of self, the denial of the will of the flesh—is part of the work Jesus did on the cross.

When people are blinded by witchcraft to the reality of the cross they lose those three dimensions. They no longer understand that God has abolished law as a means of achieving righteousness. They no longer understand that the cross represents God's estimate of our carnal nature. And they no longer apply the principle of the crucified life—denial of the flesh—to their own lives. They become carnal, self-indulgent, self-pleasing and self-satisfied.

The Great Appeal of Legalism

Legalism has one great hold on the human mind: It appeals to our human pride. That is why people enjoy it. That is why people can be passionately dedicated to a legalistic religion.

I have lived in the Middle East for years among Muslims and am familiar in some detail with the religion of Islam. I have said many times that it has never made one person happy in fourteen centuries. Not one person. It is a religion of misery, of rigidity, of slavery. Why then are Muslims so passionately dedicated to it? Because it appeals to their pride. They can quote you all that they have done to earn the approval of Allah.

This practice is not limited to Muslims, of course. It is a feature of nearly all religious people. We grow proud of our good works, and we become like Cain who offered to God the fruit of the ground, which God had cursed. That is a picture of our old nature in operation. Our old nature is under the curse of God, and whatever we give Him from it is an offering from something that He has declared cursed. There is no way that it will ever be acceptable to God.

Paul says many times: "We are saved by grace, not by works lest anyone should boast" (see Ephesians 2:8–9). You will find this statement at least three or four times in the New Testament. I always thought, *Why say "lest anyone should boast"?* Then it suddenly dawned on me: People like legalism because it gives them something to boast about. It is like the Pharisee who said, "I fast twice a week; I give tithes of all that I possess. I don't commit adultery or extortion or injustice" (see Luke 18:11–12). But he was not justified. If we think we can offer to God something acceptable out of our old fallen nature, we are telling God, in effect, that Jesus did not need to die.

Paul says that if righteousness can come through law, then Christ died to no effect (see Galatians 2:21). And when we say that to God we incur His disfavor, because anything we do to dishonor Jesus incurs the disfavor of God. It does not mean God will banish us from His presence, but we cannot live in His favor while we are in any way undermining what Jesus accomplished on the cross.

Here is an interesting fact: Paul wrote to a number of different churches—the Romans, the Corinthians, the Colossians, the Ephesians and so on. In almost every one of the letters he began by thanking God for the people he was writing to, even the Corinthians. In Corinth, one man was living with his father's wife, and there was drunkenness at the Lord's Table. But Paul still thanked God for His grace to His people.

But when he wrote to the Galatians, he was so upset he left that out. His first sentence is, "I marvel that you are so soon moved from the grace of God." They were not committing adultery there. They were not getting drunk. What was their problem? Legalism. And this was far more serious in Paul's eyes than those obvious sins of the flesh that religious people are so quick to condemn.

The Consequences of Legalism

Let us see then the consequences on our call and accomplishing our Kingdom assignments when witchcraft entices God's people into legalism.

First of all, any of God's people who are blinded by witchcraft to the work of the cross are relying on their own efforts and are put back under law.

Second, legalism leaves no room for God's supernatural. Paul said this about miracles: "Do they come by observing the law or do they come by the hearing of faith?" (see Galatians 3:5). Of course, the answer is that miracles come by the hearing of faith. When the church becomes legalistic under the influence of witchcraft, it loses any demonstration of the supernatural. The problem is legalism because God will not grant the supernatural to the efforts of the fleshly nature. They never qualify. The next step in this degeneration is that theologians begin to tell us that God has withdrawn the supernatural—it was only for the apostolic age. First we sin by rejecting the supernatural and then we compound our sin by explaining that God has taken it away. That is a lie—a theological lie—a cover-up for our own failure.

Third, going back under the law brings a curse. Instead of being in the blessing of God we find ourselves under the curse of God.

Let's go a little further down in Galatians where we read:

> As many as are of the works of the law [or simply "law"] are under the curse; for it is written, "Cursed is everyone who does not continue in all things which are written in the book of the law, to do them."
>
> Galatians 3:10

You see, if you are going to be justified by the law, you have to keep the *whole* law *all the time*. You cannot choose little bits of the law to keep and not worry about the rest. The law is an entire, single system. Either you observe *all* of it *all* of the time or it is of no benefit for you in achieving righteousness with God.

> That no one is justified by the law in the sight of God is evident, for "the just shall live by faith." Yet the law is not of faith, but "the man who does them shall live by them." Christ has redeemed us from the curse of the law, having become a curse for us (for it is written, "Cursed is everyone who hangs on a tree").
>
> verses 11–13

You notice the word *curse* occurs three times in that last verse. What is the cause of the curse? The law. How do we come under the curse? By going back from grace and from the supernatural (which always goes with grace), and by relying on our own efforts.

You may say, "Well, that was the Law of Moses." True, Paul had that in mind. But there is a curse pronounced in the book of Jeremiah that concerns all of us: "Thus says the LORD: 'Cursed is the man who trusts in man and makes flesh his strength, whose heart departs from the LORD'" (Jeremiah 17:5).

When we rely on our own fleshly ability we have come under a curse. "Cursed is the man who trusts in man." How many churches are filled with people who trust in man? That includes trusting in yourself. The Bible says the one who does this is under a curse. Why? Because that person's heart "departs from the Lord."

Basically, I would say that is the history of the Christian Church. God visits His people and they experience His grace and His supernatural power. But very rarely does it last more than one generation. Then they turn away into self-effort, human rules and human systems.

Falling into Serious Error

What is the basic error in legalism? This is important because the basic error is a serious one. The basic error is rejecting the Holy Spirit. We no longer rely on the Spirit of God. And when we reject the Holy Spirit, we create a vacuum that is filled by the spirit of witchcraft. It is a matter of cause and effect.

My own inexpert summation of Church history is that for nearly twenty centuries we have been trying to find a system so safe we do not have to trust the Holy Spirit. Unfortunately, there is no such system. And the riskiest thing you can ever do in the long run is cease trusting the Holy Spirit.

Religious leaders are afraid of anything they cannot themselves control. But anything that religious leaders *can* control does not have the power to do what is needed. If we settle for what we can control, we are settling for something that God will not accept. Many people feel it is dangerous to rely on the Holy Spirit. In a certain sense, it is. You could draw wrong conclusions, for instance, and be wrong in your actions. It has happened before. But I want to tell you, it is much more dangerous not to rely on the Holy Spirit. The third Person of the Godhead is very gracious, very patient and very gentle. But if we persistently say, "Thank You, but we don't need You," we have insulted Him and that is the way to disaster.

When we seek to achieve righteousness by law, we are releasing the fleshly nature. That is why so many problems arise from legalistic people. It was the legalists who crucified Jesus and the apostles, not the harlots or the tax collectors. I will tell you unequivocally that God's biggest problem is religious people. We see this clearly stated in Romans 7:5: "For when we were in the flesh, the sinful passions which were aroused by the law were at work in our members to bear fruit to death."

Why are the sinful passions aroused? Because when I am operating by the law, I say, "I'll do it." I am really relying on my own carnal nature. When I rely on my carnal nature, I release what is in my carnal nature. What is in the carnal nature? The answer is in the Scripture that follows, and I will tell you in advance, it is not a pretty picture. Here is what is released the moment we begin to rely on our own natural ability and righteousness:

> The works of the flesh are evident, which are: adultery, for-
> nication, uncleanness, lewdness, idolatry, sorcery [notice that

sorcery is one of the works of the flesh], hatred, contentions, jealousies, outbursts of wrath, selfish ambitions, dissensions, heresies, envy, murders, drunkenness, revelries, and the like; of which I tell you beforehand, just as I also told you in time past, that those who practice such things will not inherit the kingdom of God.

Galatians 5:19–21

The words in this list differ slightly according to the translation used, but there are really four categories of the works of the flesh. The first is *sexual immorality* (adultery, fornication, uncleanness). The second is the realm of the *occult* and *false religion* (idolatry, sorcery). The third is *licentious living* (drunkenness, reveling and the like). The fourth and major category is *every form of strife and division*. That is why churches divide. The real issue is not doctrine or theology, but the fleshly nature. The fleshly nature cannot get along with itself, let alone with a brother or a sister in the Lord. As soon as Christians become carnal in their thinking and their attitudes, you can be sure that their church is headed for division.

Why do so many denominations have so many different varieties? Why do they split so often? Because of their intense legalism that releases these ugly works of the flesh. Christians may stay away from drunkenness and immorality, but they do not seem to be able to stay away from strife and bitterness and hatred.

God gives grace to the humble—not to those who insist on being right.

Where Your Dependence Belongs

The key to success as you seek and fulfill your calling is learning to stop depending on yourself. You are not dependable. The most important lesson you can learn in the Christian life is how to maintain a continuing, moment-by-moment dependence on the Holy Spirit. In a word, never make a decision toward your calling or any Kingdom work without the Holy Spirit.

I remember a significant time when the Lord spoke to me through a prophecy. He told me that I would be entering a new phase in my ministry, and that I would be walking a way that I had never walked before. He said, *You're going to have to be extremely sensitive. Don't go one step ahead of Me. Don't speak one syllable before Me.* It reinforced the realization that this dependence on the Holy Spirit is what leads to success. But that is not to say that it is easy for me. By nature, I am an independent person. I made my own way in life and in many ways I am successful. One of my closest friends said of me that I am the most self-dependent man he ever met, and I would not deny that assessment. The greatest, perhaps the most persistent, challenge in my Christian life has been to stop depending on myself.

Here is an example of an issue I struggle with: I tend to say anything when it comes into my mind, but that is not always the right time to say it. I may be engaged in a conversation and about to say something when the Holy Spirit says, *It isn't the time to say that.* If I am depending on the Holy Spirit, I will take heed of what He says and wait. It takes patience to wait. Do you pray for patience? You do well. But just remember that God has His ways of teaching us patience. The old King James word for *patience* is *longsuffering*, and generally we learn longsuffering by suffering long.

I am sure you have felt the Holy Spirit's little gentle nudges along these lines. Suppose you are taking a car trip. When you get into your car, do you sense that He wants you to pray? Being in a car today is being in a dangerous place. There is a high probability of having an accident. Do you ask God's protection? Do you buckle your seat belt? I have known several dear brothers in the Lord who had serious injuries in automobile accidents simply because they were not wearing seat belts.

Over the years I have learned not to get frustrated when things do not go the way I want. I have learned that God often has a reason for this. Our response to such situations needs to be, "Holy Spirit, show me." I know I have not arrived, but I do want a good relationship with the Holy Spirit. I have come to the place where I have no confidence in my flesh. I know it will not produce anything that I would want.

Release from Legalism

The Law of Moses that God gave to Israel was an absolutely perfect map. Paul is insistent upon that fact. He says the law is "holy and just and good" (Romans 7:12). If anybody had followed that map exactly he would have achieved perfect righteousness. But the law could not achieve righteousness, and the reason is the weakness of our carnal nature. The Bible reveals that every one of us is born with an inner problem, which is rebellion against God. When we set our will to keep the law, this rebel in us rises up and frustrates our most sincere efforts. If we take steps into legalism, we come under spiritual bondage to the evil force of witchcraft.

In my own experience, when I saw what my real condition was I realized that it was not enough just to change my mind. I had to repent and ask God to release me from the spiritual bondage of legalism and rebellion. I do not mean to say that this is the unforgivable sin, but in many cases we slight or insult the Holy Spirit.

A strange example comes to my mind from my days at Cambridge. Another student, whose name was Smithers, was an anarchist by philosophy and by conviction. He wore a black, straggly beard, which was unusual in those days. He was somewhat of a marked man because of his impertinence.

On one occasion, the tutor of King's College, who was a dignified and important person, went to see Smithers to see if he needed a grant for further studies. We knew that Smithers' anarchistic principles would make it difficult for him to be polite to the tutor. So when the interview was over, we asked Smithers, "How did you behave?"

He replied, "I tried to act as if he wasn't there."

I relate this story because I think a lot of us have had the same attitude toward the Holy Spirit. We have tried to act as if He were not there. We have ignored His presence, and that is an insult. We have insulted the Spirit of grace and we need to repent. When we have repented, we need to ask God to release us from the spirit of bondage that has held many of us captive from fulfilling our callings.

Do you feel that what I have described accurately represents your basic problem? It may be a problem that you have been struggling with for years. You have tried your hardest and done your best, but your life never really seems to produce the results spoken of in the New Testament. Would you like to send a distress signal to the Holy Spirit right now? Here is what you may wish to say:

> *Holy Spirit, I'm stuck. I don't know which way to go. I can't get out. I'm sorry that I have tried to go my own way and follow my own interests without You. Please forgive me, Holy Spirit. I yield myself afresh to You. I desire spiritual union with Jesus that the Bible talks about. Will You grant that to me? Will You come to my aid?*
>
> *Holy Spirit, I'm sorry I have insulted You. I've done my best to ignore You. I have trusted in myself and in my own strength. Forgive me and deliver me from that spirit of bondage, I pray. In Jesus' name, Amen.*

What Now?

Here is an amazing fact that you may or may not have ever pondered. Immediately after God gave the covenant of the Law to Moses to give to His people Israel, a people whom He had redeemed—not by law, but by faith—out of bondage in Egypt, what was their first act? The first thing the people did was to break the first two Commandments—not to have any other god and not to worship idols.

Some teachers suggest that people break the law because it is too difficult to keep, but that is absurd in this context. It was much more difficult for them to make a golden calf and worship it than it was just to go on obeying God. Why did they sin immediately? Because the law that was given to them provoked the rebel inside them.

Left to our own efforts we can only say, "God, I can't make it. There is nothing wrong with the law. It is a perfect map. But every time I try to follow it I stumble into a bog."

Thank God He has given us a Guide—the Holy Spirit. If we offer the Holy Spirit the map, He says, *Thank you, but I already know the way. I don't need the map. All you need to do is hold My hand and let Me lead you.*

Here are two important questions for you to answer. First, at some time, have you heard the message that you must be born again? Undoubtedly, your answer is yes. So here is my second question: Have you ever had clear, practical, systematic teaching on how to be led by the Holy Spirit?

Your answers to those questions lay bare one of the root problems of the Church. Many people who have been born again have never been taught how to be led by the Spirit. They get into the Kingdom of God and they stumble around and never move into their callings. They never make any real progress toward their particular assignments that God has ordained for them in the Kingdom. Why? Because they have never received needed teaching on how to be led by the Holy Spirit.

This is the subject of our next chapter.

8

The One Who Guides You

However, when He, the Spirit of truth, has come, He will guide you into all truth.

John 16:13

There is no substitute in the whole universe for the Holy Spirit. He is absolutely unique, and He can do what no other person and no other power can do. He is the only One who can do in us what God wants to be done.

There is a Scripture in the Old Testament that says, "This is the word of the LORD to Zerubbabel: 'Not by might nor by power, but by My Spirit,' says the LORD of hosts" (Zechariah 4:6). Those last words tell us something important. The Lord of Hosts is speaking—the God who commands all the hosts of heaven and earth. He says, "Might and power cannot do what has to be done, which is to change people radically on the inside. Force will not do it. Pressure will not do it. Law will not do it. Government cannot do it. There is only one agent that can do it—the Holy Spirit."

I want you to grasp that.

If you want to enter into the calling that God has prepared for you in Christ, you must be totally dependent on the Holy Spirit. Apart from the Spirit of God you cannot do it. There is no substitute. Education won't do it. Talent won't do it. Money certainly will not do it. Nothing and no one but the Spirit of God—the Holy Spirit—can do it.

The One Way to Maturity

Paul makes this definitive statement in his letter to the Romans: "As many as are *led* by the Spirit of God, these are sons of God" (Romans 8:14, emphasis added). The only people who qualify to be sons and daughters of God are those who are led by the Holy Spirit. As we have noted, it is a tragic fact that vast numbers of people who have been born again of the Spirit of God have never learned how to be led by Him. There is no other way to grow to maturity in Christ.

In the Greek language *being led* is a continuing present tense meaning "as many as are being continually led by the Spirit of God." It is not something that happens in church on Sunday morning or when you kneel by your bed to pray. It is something that happens day by day, hour by hour and moment by moment. Those who are being continually led by the Spirit of God, they—and only they—become mature sons and daughters of God.

I had a tremendously powerful personal experience of the Holy Spirit when I came to know Jesus. Lying prostrate on the floor of an army barrack room in World War II, I experienced the power of God for well over an hour. It was a totally strange experience for me. My initial encounter with Jesus was also an encounter with the Holy Spirit and His power.

From then on, the Holy Spirit was always a reality to me. I studied about the Holy Spirit, I believed in the Holy Spirit, and when I became a preacher I preached about the Holy Spirit. I preached many, many times, "You must be born again of the Spirit." Looking back, however, I have to say with regret that the Holy Spirit for me at that time was rather like an emergency vehicle. When I was in desperate trouble, I phoned for the ambulance. The ambulance always turned up and helped me, but my relationship with the Holy Spirit was spasmodic.

Part of the problem was that I was deeply immersed in religion. As we have seen, religion and the Holy Spirit do not blend well together. If we are full of religious exercises, we automatically tend to rely on them and not on the Holy Spirit. In my early days I used a lot of spiritual language, but real spiritual content was missing from my life. To remedy that, God permitted me to go through various experiences, all of which were designed—one after the other—to make me aware of my total dependence on the Holy Spirit.

As you read this, you may be going through frustrations, problems and heartaches yourself. You may be saying, "God, why?" One very probable reason why God has permitted these problems to come into your life is to show you that you need the Holy Spirit—every day, every hour and every moment. There is no other way to succeed in the Christian life.

The Holy Spirit is totally willing. We never have to coerce Him or cajole Him. The problem—if there is a problem—is always in us, never in Him. The Scripture says, "The flesh lusts against the Spirit, and the Spirit against the flesh" (Galatians 5:17). Basically that means we simply cannot do the godly things we would like to do because of that built-in antipathy in our old carnal nature toward the Spirit. And so we have to learn not to be dictated to by our carnal nature. We have to learn to reckon our carnal nature dead through the death of Jesus on the cross. And we have to live for the Lord through the power of the Spirit.

Nobody achieves that ability instantly. Some people—and they are usually the conspicuously successful Christians—learn it quickly. These are not necessarily preachers. They may be people who are simply humble members of the Body of Christ. Often it is the intercessors who learn this lesson, the people who pray in hidden places and who are not much seen in public.

If you want to succeed in your calling, if you want to take up the Kingdom assignment for which you were made, if you want to conquer adversity and evil forces of the enemy, the lesson I am teaching you is essential. You must be led by the Holy Spirit.

Aspects of the Holy Spirit

Let's begin by looking at simple terms that describe certain aspects of the Holy Spirit.

The Holy Spirit Is a Person

The first and vital fact we need to realize is that the Holy Spirit is a Person. He is not just half a sentence we say at the end of the Apostle's Creed: "I believe in the Holy Spirit, the holy catholic church," etc. To me, it is something of a disaster that this official creed gives so few words to the third Person of the Godhead.

A remarkable quality of the Holy Spirit is that He personally is self-effacing. He never attracts attention to Himself. He always focuses attention on the Lord Jesus Christ. But the fact that He is self-effacing does not mean that we can afford to ignore Him.

Let's turn to the gospel of John to see what Jesus has to say on this matter. In the passage that follows, Jesus is telling His disciples that He is about to leave them in personal presence and return to the Father in heaven. In the process, He explains to them that He has made provision for their well-being after He leaves. This provision is another Person who will come from heaven after Jesus has returned there. The other Person, of course, is the Holy Spirit. Jesus says: "Nevertheless I tell you the truth. It is to your advantage that I go away; for if I do not go away, the Helper will not come to you; but if I depart, I will send Him to you" (John 16:7).

The words *helper, comforter* and *counselor* are all used for the Holy Spirit. The Roman Catholic version of the Bible uses the word *paraclete*. That is a transliteration of a Greek word *parakletos*, which means something like "one called in alongside." Perhaps the closest equivalent to this would be an *advocate*, which has a certain legal connotation. This portrays the Holy Spirit as somebody who is called in alongside to help you, to plead your case in the law court when you are not competent to do it. All those words describe attributes of the Holy Spirit—He is the Comforter, the Helper, the Counselor, the Advocate, the Paraclete.

Notice two points in particular. First of all, Jesus says, "I am leaving you as a Person." At this very moment as you are reading this, Jesus, as a Person, is seated at the right hand of the Father in heaven. He is not on earth. Second, when Jesus was telling His disciples, "If I go back to heaven, in My place I will ask the Father to send you *another* Person" (see John 14:16), that word *another* is particularly important. Why? Because it emphasizes that the Holy Spirit is just as much a Person as Jesus Himself and as the Father.

The New Testament particularly, and the whole Bible in fact, reveals the triune nature of God—one God in three Persons: Father, Son and Holy Spirit. Each of those three expressions of the Godhead is a Person. It has been my observation that we have no difficulty understanding that the Father is a Person and that the Son is a Person, but it seems that many people find it hard to comprehend that the Spirit is just as much a Person, although a Person of a somewhat different kind.

In the same chapter of John, a little further on, Jesus says, "When He, the Spirit of truth, has come, He will guide you into all truth" (John 16:13).

The Greek language, in which the New Testament has come to us, is a language with genders—masculine, feminine and neuter. We have very little of that differentiation in English, although we have the three pronouns *he*, *she* and *it*. But English is not like French, for instance, which makes *ceiling* masculine and *door* feminine. Those are what we call grammatical genders.

In the Greek language, the word for Spirit, *pneuma*, is neither masculine nor feminine—but neuter. The appropriate pronoun for the neuter gender would be *it*. But these recorded words that Jesus speaks to His disciples break the laws of grammar to use another pronoun. He does not say *it*. He says, "When *He*, the Spirit of truth, has come." Why does Jesus do that? To leave no possible doubt that the Holy Spirit is a Person. The Holy Spirit is not an *it*. The Holy Spirit is not an influence or a doctrine or a theological abstraction. He is a Person.

That is a vital truth for us to grasp. If you do not understand it, you will always have problems relating to Him. In the same way, I would have problems relating to my wife if I did not realize she was a person. Our marriage would be on the rocks. Just so, many people have a very uneasy relationship with the Holy Spirit because they have not grasped the fact that He is a Person.

The Holy Spirit Is Present

The second point I want you to notice is that Jesus says to His disciples, "It is to your advantage that I should go away, because if I don't go, the Helper won't come. But if I go, I'll send Him in My place" (see John 16:7). What Jesus is saying here surprises many Christians. He is saying, "You'll be better off with Me in heaven and the Holy Spirit on earth than you are with Me on earth and the Holy Spirit in heaven."

You may have said to yourself at one time or another, "Wouldn't it have been wonderful to be there in the days when Jesus was on earth? Then we could actually have fellowship with Him in His human nature." Yes, it *would* have been wonderful! But in this verse, Jesus is saying, "Nevertheless, you are much better off now with Me in heaven and the Spirit on earth."

If you study the history of the development of the Church, the truth of what Jesus is saying is obvious. The day the Holy Spirit came—the Day of Pentecost—the disciples were transformed in a way they had never been transformed in all the time that Jesus was with them. Even up to the last moments during the Last Supper they were quarrelling among themselves about which of them should be the greatest. Half of the profound truths Jesus was sharing about His death and resurrection seemed lost on them.

But the moment the Holy Spirit came, they had a totally different grasp of the identity of Jesus. They had an instantaneous awareness of the reality and meaning of His death and resurrection, and of the Scriptures. Before the Day of Pentecost, Peter could never have stood up and applied the prophecy of Joel to what they had just experienced. That insight did not come gradually; it came instantly. The moment the Holy Spirit came, their attitude and their grasp of spiritual truths were revolutionized instantly.

The Holy Spirit Is Lord

The third vital fact concerning the Holy Spirit is an extension of the first. Not only is the Holy Spirit a Person, but He is Lord. Just as God the Father is Lord and God the Son is Lord, so God the Spirit is Lord. He is coequal with the other two members of the Godhead. Part of the Nicene Creed states, "the Holy Spirit . . . who together with the Father and the Son is worshiped." Worship is offered only to God. In 2 Corinthians Paul makes this simple statement: "Now the Lord is the Spirit; and where the Spirit of the Lord is, there is liberty" (2 Corinthians 3:17). The phrase *the Lord* in the New Testament corresponds to the sacred name of God in the Old Testament, which is sometimes called *Jehovah*. It is the name of the one true God. So when Paul says, "The Lord is the Spirit," he is saying, "The Spirit is God; He is Lord."

Paul goes on to say, "Where the Spirit is, there is liberty." There you see the contrast between bondage to a legal system and liberty. How do we have liberty? There is only one way. Where the Holy Spirit is, there is liberty. I heard someone paraphrase that verse as follows: "Where the Holy Spirit is Lord, there is liberty."

Pentecostals, of whom I am one, and other people like them have often had the strangest ideas about liberty. Like this: If we don't start dancing on the platform by 6:45 P.M. on Sunday evening, we are not in liberty. Or this: If we don't all clap our hands, we don't have liberty. Some preachers think if they don't stamp their feet on the platform and shout they don't have liberty. True, some preachers do have liberty when they stamp on the platform and shout, but for me to do that would not be liberty.

Liberty is not a matter of following a certain program in church every Sunday. Neither is it going through certain motions. It depends on whether the Holy Spirit is prompting it or you are doing it out of a religious tradition. Religious traditions produce only bondage.

We need to have the same attitude of reverence toward the Holy Spirit that we have toward the Father and the Son. You see, we have no more access to God than what we have by the Holy Spirit, because there is a principle in the Godhead. In order to have access to the Godhead, the One who is sent as the Representative must be honored. When the Father sent the Son, He said, "From now on, no one comes to Me but through the Son. You cannot bypass My Representative and come to Me, because in every situation and circumstance, I uphold the One whom I have sent."

When Jesus had finished His task, He returned to the Father. As I understand it (this, of course, is a theological issue much more complex than one sentence can express), the Father and the Son together sent the Holy Spirit. And the same principle applies. We have no access to the Father and the Son except by the Spirit. We cannot bypass Him. Paul says in Ephesians 2: "For through Him we both [Jews and Gentiles] have access by one Spirit to the Father" (Ephesians 2:18).

Lots of evangelical Christians focus on the fact that we have access to God through the Son, Jesus. That is perfectly true, but it is not the whole truth. Our access is through the Son by the Spirit to the Father. Likewise, the Father indwells us when we are in the Son through His Spirit. In each direction, whether we are going to God or whether God is coming to us, the Spirit is an essential part of the equation. If we leave the Holy Spirit out of that equation, we have no access to God and God has no access to us. We are totally dependent on the Holy Spirit.

The Dove and the Lamb

Scripture gives us a beautiful picture of what the Holy Spirit wants in a person. He found it in only one man: Jesus.

> And John bore witness, saying, "I saw the Spirit descending from heaven like a dove, and He remained upon Him. I did not know Him, but He who sent me to baptize with water said to me, 'Upon whom you see the Spirit descending, and remaining on Him, this is He who baptizes with the Holy Spirit.' And I have seen and testified that this is the Son of God."
>
> John 1:32–34

The mark that would confirm Jesus as the Messiah was that the Holy Spirit would descend upon Him in bodily form. But that was not the most significant fact. The really significant fact was that the Holy Spirit *remained* on Him. The Holy Spirit has descended on many of us, but we have said and done things that scared Him away. Jesus never scared the Dove away.

Now look at the picture of John the Baptist introducing Jesus. "The next day John [the Baptist] saw Jesus coming toward him, and said, 'Behold! The Lamb of God who takes away the sin of the world!'" (John 1:29). John pictured Jesus as a Lamb.

In these Scriptures we see two Persons of the Godhead—the Son and the Spirit—both represented in picture form as members of the animal creation. Jesus is portrayed as a lamb; the descended Holy Spirit is portrayed in the form of a dove.

That is a beautiful representation of the truth. What is the Dove looking for? He is looking for the nature of the Lamb. Where He finds the nature of the Lamb, He will not merely come down, but He will stay. I believe the kind of dove represented here is the beautiful pure white bird. Interestingly enough, it is one of the few birds that can focus with both eyes on a single object. On the whole, it is a timid bird, easily scared away. All of which shows us that we need to be sensitive to the Holy Spirit.

Many years ago, about 1946, in Jerusalem, I was teaching a children's church in the home we occupied there. Our meetings were held on the first floor in a large entrance hall and the pulpit was in front of a door that opened onto a veranda. I was standing behind the pulpit with my back to the door. On the veranda behind me we happened to have a round table with what we were using as a tablecloth—an Arab woman's black shawl—upon it. That day I was teaching the children about the Holy Spirit. I was telling them the Holy Spirit is like a dove and that if we want the dove to stay with us, we have to be very careful not to say or do anything that would scare Him away.

As I was teaching, I noticed that the children's attention was riveted on me. They became absolutely motionless. Their eyes were round and big and focused in my direction. I have never had such attention from a group of children. Without my knowing it, a beautiful white dove had alighted in the center of that black tablecloth and was standing there. Of course, the white of the dove against the black of the shawl was a dramatic picture. The children were so attentive because they were desperately afraid they would do something to scare the dove away.

That was one sermon of mine that the Lord Himself chose to illustrate. That truth stayed with me, because of what I saw in the rapt attention of those children. I thought to myself, *If only we could understand that the Holy Spirit is like that, how careful we would be in our attitudes and our relationships to Him.*

Attributes of the Nature of a Lamb

Let's focus our attention now on the nature of the Lamb. In the Bible, a lamb represents certain qualities that would attract the Holy Spirit: purity, meekness and a life laid down in sacrifice. Do you want to have the Holy Spirit continually with you? These are the attributes you need to cultivate: purity, meekness and a life that is not being lived for yourself—a life that is laid down for Christ and for His Body. Then the Dove will settle on you and you will not scare Him away.

Jesus attributed His whole ministry to the presence of the Holy Spirit. He never took the credit for what He did. When Jesus was in the synagogue in His home city, Nazareth, He was handed the book of the prophet Isaiah:

> And when He had opened the book, He found the place where it was written: "The Spirit of the LORD is upon Me, because He has anointed Me to preach the gospel to the poor; He has sent Me to heal the brokenhearted, to proclaim liberty to the captives and recovery of sight to the blind, to set at liberty those who are oppressed; to proclaim the acceptable year of the LORD."
>
> Luke 4:17–19

If we wish to continue with that message and that ministry as we move forward in our callings, we are under the same condition as the Lord Jesus. It is only possible by the anointing of the Holy Spirit. John Wesley quoted those words in one of his journals and said, "I suppose that these words are true of every man who has been truly called to proclaim the gospel." There is no other way that we can have any success except by the anointing of the Holy Spirit.

The success of any calling is in exact proportion to the measure of the anointing of the Holy Spirit. If Jesus could not do it without the Holy Spirit, be very sure that you and I cannot.

Paul writes:

> Do not grieve the Holy Spirit of God [do not scare the Dove away], by whom you were sealed for the day of redemption. [And then he gives a list of things that scare the Dove:] Let all bitterness, wrath, anger, clamor, and evil speaking be put away from you, with all malice.
>
> Ephesians 4:30–31

Paul ends with the following qualities that the Dove looks for: "And be kind to one another, tenderhearted, forgiving one another, even as God in Christ forgave you" (verse 32). These qualities are our responsibility. This is the way to attract the Holy Spirit and have Him remain on us.

Do Not Go Back

What, then, is the ultimate function of the Holy Spirit? I believe it is through the Holy Spirit that we are united with Christ. Galatians 5:18 tells us this: "If you are led by the Spirit, you are not under the law." In the flesh, we were under the law. Jesus died for our fleshly nature, that our nature in Him might be reckoned dead. After we are reckoned dead, we can be united to the resurrected Christ in a union that Paul compares with marriage—something that might perhaps scare religious people, but the Bible does not hesitate to use the most intense and passionate language about our relationship to Jesus.

Do not rely on rules or the religious system to advance you in your calling. The Holy Spirit will not share with any system. When Isaac comes, Ishmael has to go. They will not live in the same house.

William Booth's daughter, Kate Booth-Clibborn, who brought The Salvation Army to France, once said this: "Christ loves us passionately and He wants to be loved passionately." Many of us need a much more passionate devotion to Jesus, and we can only have it through the Holy Spirit. He will give us that marriage union with the resurrected Christ.

I believe our union with Jesus is consummated by worship. When we, by the Holy Spirit, worship the resurrected Christ, we come into union with Him. "Do you not know," Paul said, "that he who is joined to a harlot [prostitute] is one body with her? . . . But he who is joined to the Lord is one spirit with Him" (1 Corinthians 6:16–17). Just as a person's body can be united with the body of a prostitute, so the spirit of the believer is united with the Spirit of God through the Holy Spirit. God seeks those who will worship Him in Spirit and in truth.

This brings us to the need for transformation in our lives, our lifestyles and our attitudes. With the Holy Spirit's help, we can begin to see ourselves as we really are, and take the steps toward freedom we need to take.

9

Your "Self" Must Cooperate

Oh, what a terrible predicament I'm in! Who will free me
from my slavery to this deadly lower nature? Thank God! It
has been done by Jesus Christ our Lord. He has set me free.

Romans 7:24–25, TLB

Two unnamed persons occupy a position of unique importance
in the total revelation of the New Testament. In fact, it would
be correct to say that you can never properly understand the message
of the New Testament, not to mention its application to your calling and your growth in the Kingdom, until you become thoroughly
acquainted with these two persons—their origin, their nature and
their destiny. Who are they? In the rather picturesque language of
the King James Version the two persons are *the old man* and *the new
man*. In modern translations they are called *the old self* and *the new self*.

In his letter to the Ephesian church, Paul said this: "You did not
learn Christ in this way, if indeed you have heard Him and have
been taught in Him, just as truth is in Jesus" (Ephesians 4:20–21,
NASB). It is significant to note that Paul is writing to committed
Christians, yet he leaves open the possibility that they may not have

heard the truth God wants them to hear concerning their position in Jesus. The same is true today for many sincere Christians. They have not heard the truth about the old self and the new self.

> That, in reference to your former manner of life, you lay aside the old self, which is being corrupted in accordance with the lusts of deceit, and that you be renewed in the spirit of your mind, and put on the new self, which in the likeness of God has been created in righteousness and holiness of the truth.
>
> Ephesians 4:22–24, NASB

Scripture requires that we take specific action about these two *selves*:

1. *Put off* the old self
2. *Put on* the new self

Obviously, if we are going to be able to do this, we must identify both the old self and the new self. Let's begin with the origin and nature of the old self, summed up in the words of Paul: "The old self . . . is being corrupted in accordance with the lusts of deceit."

This passage holds three key words: *corruption*, *lust* and *deceit*. We begin with the word *deceit*. The old self is the product of deceit or deception—specifically, Satan's deception. In a word, the old self is the result of man heeding Satan's lie.

In order to understand the full nature of the lie, we have to go back to the record of man's creation and the origin of human history. You will recall that after Adam and Eve had been created, God warned them not to eat from one particular tree in the Garden—the Tree of Knowledge of Good and Evil. God gave them a solemn promise: "In the day that you eat from it you will surely die" (Genesis 2:17, NASB).

In the next chapter of Genesis we read that Satan, in the form of the serpent, came to the woman, Eve, and tempted her. In essence, his temptation was for her to ignore God's warning and to disobey what God had told her and her husband. In persuading Eve to do this, Satan brought forth his lie, *the* lie.

God had said, "You will surely die."

Satan said, "You surely will not die!" (Genesis 3:4, NASB).

That was a direct lie! That negation of God's truth gave birth to the old self. The old self is, then, the product of deception, Satan's lie. Bear in mind that deception is Satan's primary activity against the human race. In Revelation 12:9, Satan is called "the great dragon . . . that serpent of old, called the Devil and Satan, who deceives the whole world."

Deception sets in motion a process of degeneration. The book of James tells us that deception produces *lust*. Lust is a perverted, rebellious desire—desire that is contrary to the will of God and contrary to the well-being of the one who entertains that desire. Lust, in turn, produces sin. And sin produces death.

> Let no one say when he is tempted, "I am being tempted by God"; for God cannot be tempted by evil, and He Himself does not tempt anyone. But each one is tempted when he is carried away and enticed by his own lust. Then when lust has conceived, it gives birth to sin; and when sin is accomplished, it brings forth death.
>
> James 1:13–15, NASB

The old man is *corrupt* in every area—spiritually, morally and physically. The old man is, in fact, the offspring of Satan. In Genesis 3:15, immediately after man's disobedience, the Lord spoke to the serpent and spoke about the serpent's seed: "I will put enmity between you and the woman, and between your seed and her Seed; He shall bruise your head, and you shall bruise His heel." The old self is that offspring or seed of Satan because it reproduces the nature of Satan.

Jesus said to the religious leaders of His day, "You are of your father the devil" (John 8:44). The devil is the father of the children of disobedience and his nature is reproduced in them. Satan's nature can be summed up in one word: *rebellion*. He is the leader of all rebellion in the universe. Hence, the behavior of the old nature is inevitably rebellious behavior, as Scripture verifies: "All of us like sheep have gone astray, each of us has turned to his own way"

(Isaiah 53:6, NASB). The mark of the old nature is that it turns to its own way. It turns its back on God and seeks its own will, pleasure and satisfaction.

This fact is described in greater detail in Ephesians where Paul says this:

> And you were dead in your trespasses and sins, in which you formerly walked according to the course of this world, according to the prince of the power of the air [Satan], of the spirit that is now working in the sons of disobedience. Among them we too all formerly lived in the lusts of our flesh, indulging the desires of the flesh and of the mind, and were by nature children of wrath, even as the rest.
>
> Ephesians 2:1–3, NASB

Notice that phrase "by nature children of wrath." Why are we objects of wrath? Because by nature we are "sons of disobedience" and disobedience always brings down God's wrath. So we have in us a corrupt, rebellious nature that is the product of Satan's deception and of lust. To sum it up: There is a rebel inside each one of us. In Scripture that rebel is called "the old man."

Human Solutions

Humans generally try to deal with this rebellion in ways that are not God's solution. First of all, we can rule out all the solutions beginning with self, many of which seem to multiply daily in contemporary psychology and thought—self-realization, self-fulfillment, self-expression. Why rule them out? Because all of these "solutions" give rein to a self that is a rebel. We have passed through a few generations that decided it was wrong to discipline or restrain children—that they should be granted freedom of self-expression. I believe those generations have learned, alas too late, that what they were doing was giving freedom of expression to a rebel.

Second, God's solution is *not* a system of law. Many people look to law to deal with the problem of the old self. But the failure of Israel, to whom the Law of Moses was given, is a demonstration that law does not achieve the desired end. The reason is not that there is anything wrong with law. Law is good in itself, as Paul says in Romans 7, but it cannot change the rebel. And anything that does not change the rebel is not a permanent solution.

Third, God's solution for the old self is *not* religion. Religion is somewhat like a refrigerator. It can temporarily conceal corruption or arrest it, but it cannot ultimately change it. Take, for example, a luscious peach. It looks so fresh and appetizing—and yet, left to itself, it will quickly wither because the process of corruption is already at work in it. It is possible to arrest the process of corruption for a little while by putting that peach in the refrigerator. But ultimately, even in the refrigerator, it will rot.

God's Solution

God's solution for the old self can be summed up in one familiar word: execution. God does not send the old self to church or to the psychiatrist. He does not improve him, He does not reform him, He does not make him religious. God executes the old self. There is no other solution for that rebel. But the Good News of the Gospel is that the execution has already taken place in Christ! This is the key to understanding the Gospel message.

Paul says that Jesus has set us free (see Romans 7:24–25). How has Jesus set us free? "Our old self was crucified with him so that the body of sin might be done away with, that we should no longer be slaves to sin" (Romans 6:6, NIV).

The only way of escape from the slavery of sin is to know and believe that our old self, that deadly lower nature, was crucified with Jesus. When Jesus died on the cross, that rebel, the old self, was executed in Him.

A good many years ago, about the time of Easter, I had in my mind a picture of the hill of Calvary—or Golgotha—with three crosses upon it. The central cross was outstanding. It was higher than the other two on either side. As this scene was before my mind, the Holy Spirit spoke to me. He asked me a question: *For whom was the center cross made?* And then it was as though He added, *Be careful. Think before you answer.*

So I thought it over and I gave this answer, "The center cross was made for Barabbas." That is a fact. Barabbas was due to be executed on that center cross, but at the last moment by divine providence, an exchange was made and Jesus took his place.

Then the Holy Spirit said to me, *If the center cross was made for Barabbas, and Jesus was crucified on that center cross, then Jesus took the place of Barabbas.*

And I replied, "Yes, that's right."

Then the Holy Spirit said to me, *But I thought Jesus took your place.*

And I said, "Yes, He did."

Then the Holy Spirit said, *Then you must be Barabbas.*

At that moment, I realized it—with a flash of insight. It is a spiritual truth that I never argue about. I simply admit it. God's Word states it clearly, but it is only the Holy Spirit who can help us to see: *You're the criminal! Your old self is the criminal, the one for whom that cross was legitimately made. It was made according to your specifications. It fits you exactly. It's where you ought to be.*

But here is the glorious and wonderful message of the Gospel of God's mercy. At the last moment, an exchange was made. Jesus took the place of Barabbas—the old self.

How Then Do We Live?

In that substitution, Christ gave Himself for us. He was identified with our rebellion and He paid the penalty of the rebel. He was executed under God's judgment in our place. Because it was an exchange, Paul sees not only Jesus' identification with us, but our identification with Jesus. He states it in these words:

> I have been crucified with Christ; it is no longer I who live, but Christ lives in me; and the life which I now live in the flesh I live by faith in the Son of God, who loved me and gave Himself for me.
>
> Galatians 2:20

"When Christ died, I died," Paul declares. "That was my death." And then Paul goes on to say, "As a consequence, I no longer live." If that is true, then how is he still alive? Paul's answer is simple and direct: "Christ lives in me."

Each of us can say what Paul is saying: "It is now Christ living out His life in me. It is no longer my old, rebellious, fallen nature that is at work. Instead, it is the new nature, the divine nature of Jesus, working out in me the righteousness of Jesus, enabling me to live an entirely different kind of life."

Paul later restates this same principle in his letter to the Colossians, writing to Christian believers: "For you died, and your life is hidden with Christ in God. When Christ who is our life appears, then you also will appear with Him in glory" (Colossians 3:3–4). When did we die? We died when Jesus died; that was our death. We have our own lives no longer—we have a hidden life, a secret life, a life that this world, which is restricted to the senses, cannot appreciate or understand.

Again, we can say with Paul, "It is no longer I who live, but Christ who lives in me. The life I live now—in this present age, in this present body—I live by faith in the Son of God who loved me and gave Himself for me." Here then is the wonderful truth the Scriptures declare: We have passed from death to life.

Burial and Resurrection

Because of this magnificent exchange that takes us from death to life, another exchange takes place. We become identified with Jesus in all that followed His death: burial and resurrection. Look at the comprehensive summation of the Gospel given by Paul in 1 Corinthians:

> Moreover, brethren, I declare to you the gospel which I preached to you, which also you received and in which you stand, by which also you are saved, if you hold fast that word which I preached to you—unless you believed in vain. For I delivered to you first of all that which I also received: that Christ died for our sins according to the Scriptures, and that

He was buried, and that He rose again the third day according
to the Scriptures.

1 Corinthians 15:1–4

Paul states here the essence of the Gospel. It centers on Christ
and contains three successive statements. First of all, Christ died;
second, He was buried; third, He was raised on the third day. That
is the absolute heart and essence of the Gospel, and it does not
depend on any additional human contributions or embellishments.

In Paul's time and context, "according to the Scriptures"
meant *according to the Old Testament*. We may well ask, "Where
does it say in the Old Testament that Jesus would be raised on the
third day?" I wonder if you have ever considered that question. It
puzzled me for many years, but I believe that God showed me the
answer.

First of all, Jesus said that He would be like Jonah of the Old
Testament. We know that Jonah was three days in the belly of the
fish. In similar fashion, Jesus said He would be three days in the
belly of the earth. That is a pictorial presentation, but the only place
I know of in the Old Testament where this is specifically stated is
in the book of the prophet Hosea:

Come, let us return to the LORD. For He has torn us, but He
will heal us; He has wounded us, but He will bandage us. He
will revive us after two days; He will raise us up on the third
day, that we may live before Him.

Hosea 6:1–2, NASB

What has been killed will be revived. It will be brought back
to life, and it will happen after two days—on the third day.
But here is a significant point: This is all applied to us, not just to
Jesus. It does not say that God will "raise *Him* up," but that He will
"raise *us* up."

Jesus was identified with us in His death for our sin. As
we accept that identification, identify ourselves with Him in
death, and say, like Paul, "I am crucified with Christ," then the

way is open for us to be identified with Jesus in all that follows: His burial, His resurrection and even in His ascension.

In the next verse, the prophet goes on to say:

> So let us know, let us press on to know the LORD. His going forth is as certain as the dawn; and He will come to us like the rain, like the spring rain watering the earth.
>
> Hosea 6:3, NASB

We see a further picture of the resurrection of Jesus contained in the words "His going forth is as certain as the dawn." The resurrection was like the dawn after the long dark night. Next, Hosea says, "He will come to us like the rain, like the spring rain watering the earth." The spring rain and the rain coming down on the earth are used many times in the Bible as a picture of the coming down of the Holy Spirit.

So here we get a preview, not merely of the resurrection, but of that which took place fifty days after the resurrection—the coming of the Holy Spirit. This Scripture in Hosea shows us that Jesus was to die, be buried and raised the third day. But it also tells us that we are to be identified with Him in death, burial and resurrection from the dead. The promise is that if we press on to know the Lord, we will know not only the dawn of His resurrection but the rain of the coming of the Holy Spirit.

There is one specific act by which God requires us and enables us to be identified with Jesus in His death, burial and resurrection. This is the outward act of baptism. Being baptized is being buried with Christ. It is being united with Him in His death. And the Scriptures give us this guarantee: If we are united with Him in burial, then we will also follow through with Him into resurrection, into a new life (see Romans 6:3–5; Colossians 2:12).

Rebirth into a New Way of Life

In a natural birth, the head should come forth first. When the head emerges, we know the body is going to follow. So it is in this spiritual birth. In His birth out of death, Jesus, the Head of the Body, emerged first. What does that tell us? That we who are united with Him as our Head will follow Him in that birth into the new order of creation. We will follow Him into the fullness that He entered through His death and resurrection from the dead.

With Jesus as our Head, we, as the members of His Body, who are united with Him, follow Him in rebirth. We follow Him out of death into a totally new order, a totally new life—a union with Him that takes us wherever He goes. That connection to Jesus takes us not only into resurrection, but into ascension into heaven's glory, and into the place of authority at God's right hand. Listen to how Peter expresses this:

> Blessed be the God and Father of our Lord Jesus Christ, who according to His great mercy has caused us to be born again to a living hope through the resurrection of Jesus Christ from the dead, to obtain an inheritance which is imperishable and undefiled and will not fade away, reserved in heaven for you.
>
> 1 Peter 1:3–4, NASB

This is birth out of the old order into a new order, into a new way of life, into a new kind of life. In the above passage from Peter, three words describe this new order, all of which far surpass the old order of life that is familiar to us. This inheritance is *imperishable* and *undefiled* and *will not fade away*. It cannot be touched by corruption, by decay, by the contamination of sin. It cannot be defiled. It will never fade. It is not subject to all the evil, corrupting forces that we have been familiar with.

This new inheritance is not at all like the old order, which pulled us down all through our lives and defeated us. We have passed out of that realm into a new realm in Jesus through identification with Him. We have been born again to a living hope.

As we understand more fully this one glorious truth, that Jesus died our death that we might enter fully into His life, then we will find ourselves headed into not just a new life, but a life that is totally different. In the old order of things it seemed as though our callings were unknowable, unreachable. In the new order we pass out of that defeat. We see and fulfill our Kingdom assignments because we understand our identification with Jesus. We can say, as Paul says, "Oh, what a terrible predicament I'm in! Who will free me from my slavery to this deadly lower nature? Thank God! It has been done by Jesus Christ our Lord. He has set me free."

10

The New Self

Where You Are Headed

Consider yourselves to be dead to sin, but alive to God in Christ Jesus.

Romans 6:11, NASB

As John the Baptist said about Jesus, "He must increase, but I must decrease" (John 3:30, NASB). It is a principle for all of us. He, Jesus (the new self), must increase, but I (the old self) must decrease. Only in proportion as the old self decreases can the new self increase. There has to be a death before there can be freedom to walk in the calling of new life.

Even so, the old man is not going to give up without a fight. We must deal with him in two stages. The first is that we accept by faith what God says about the old man: "Our old man was crucified with Him" (Romans 6:6). That is a fact of history stated in the Word of God. We have to accept it by faith. We accept the record of Scripture that the execution took place in Jesus when He died on the cross. Our faith lays hold of the statements of the Word of God and we consider ourselves to be dead. We consider the old self to be dead, to be executed, and we consider ourselves to be alive to God in Christ Jesus. We affirm the life and the operation of the new self.

Second, the process that Paul describes has to be acted out progressively. We reckon it to be true once and for all, but we work it out in our daily living. Paul goes on to say:

> Therefore do not let sin reign in your mortal body so that you obey its lusts, and do not go on presenting the members of your body to sin as instruments of unrighteousness; but present yourselves to God as those alive from the dead, and your members as instruments of righteousness to God.
>
> Romans 6:12–13, NASB

The old self will try to go on acting as if he still has rights and as if we still have to yield to him and let him have his way. We must continue to deny the demands of the old self. Jesus said the first step in following Him is to deny ourselves, and to deny means to say no. So every time the old self tries to reassert itself and act up and take control, we say, "No. You have no claims. You're dead. I will not yield to you."

On the positive side, we present ourselves to the Holy Spirit. We yield our members—every part of our bodies and our personalities—to Him. We must allow the Holy Spirit to come in and take control. When we do, the result is obedience. That is the way the new man operates—by obedience, by yielding. The new self is the opposite of the rebel, which was expressed in disobedience.

Paul tells us, "Be renewed in the spirit of your mind, and put on the new self, which in the likeness of God has been created in righteousness and holiness of the truth" (Ephesians 4:23–24, NASB).

We learn several things from this that help us progress in our obedience. First, the new self is produced by a creative act of God. It is not something that man can ever produce by his own efforts—by religion or good works or legalism. Next, the creative act of God proceeds out of the truth; that is, the truth of God's Word. It is exactly opposite to the old self, which is the product of Satan's lie. In addition, the nature of the new self is described in two words:

righteousness and *holiness*. And finally, Paul says that the new self is in the likeness of God or, as is stated in most Bible margins alongside this verse, according to the purpose of God. Both of these are legitimate and I believe Paul includes both meanings. The new self is created according to God's original purpose for man and in the new self, God's likeness is restored.

In Colossians Paul gives us further direction:

> Do not lie to one another, since you laid aside the old self with its evil practices, and have put on the new self who is being renewed to a true knowledge according to the image of the One who created him.
>
> Colossians 3:9–10, NASB

There we see both sides of the coin: God's program for the old self and God's program for the new self. To help us grasp the origin, nature, purpose and response of the new man, here are four questions we will consider in this chapter:

How is the new self produced?
How do we bring this new person within us to maturity?
What is God's program for the new man?
What is our ultimate responsibility?

The Starting Place

How is the new self produced? The gospel of John gives us a statement about the origin of the new man:

> But as many as received Him [Jesus], to them He gave the right to become children of God, even to those who believe in His name, who were born, not of blood nor of the will of the flesh nor of the will of man, but of God.
>
> John 1:12–13, NASB

The new man is produced by a birth. In John 3:5 Jesus describes this new birth as being "born of water and the Spirit." Peter tells

121

us this: "You have been born again not of seed which is perishable but imperishable, that is, through the living and enduring word of God" (1 Peter 1:23, NASB).

This imperishable seed is, first, God's written Word. It is divine, incorruptible and eternal. The nature that it brings forth is likewise divine, incorruptible and eternal. In other words, as we receive the written Word by faith and obey it, God's Spirit brings forth within us the very nature of God—divine, incorruptible, eternal.

This imperishable seed also refers to Jesus Himself, the Word made flesh. In John 1:1, the title "the Word" of God is used three times in the one verse: "In the beginning was the Word, and the Word was with God, and the Word was God" (NASB). That refers to the One who was manifested in time and in human flesh as Jesus of Nazareth. In Revelation we are given a description of Jesus returning to earth in glory and power to reign: "He is clothed with a robe dipped in blood, and His name is called The Word of God" (Revelation 19:13, NASB).

The Gospel is the preached Word of God and Jesus is the living Word of God. There is a direct relationship between the two. When we receive and believe the preached Word, it acts like a seed. That seed brings forth in us, by an operation of the Holy Spirit, through our obedience, a new nature. This new nature is like the seed that brought it forth—it is divine, eternal and imperishable or incorruptible. The old self is essentially corrupt. The new self is incorruptible, producing in us the very nature of God's Son, Jesus Christ.

Exposing Our Minds to Truth

How do we bring this new self to maturity, fulfilling God's purposes in us? Returning once more to Ephesians 4, we see that between "[laying] aside the old self" (verse 22, NASB) and "[putting] on the new self" (verse 24, NASB), Paul says there is something that we need to do. We must "be renewed in the spirit of [our] mind[s]" (verse 23, NASB). Something has to happen in our minds—a total change in the way we think.

This can only be accomplished by the Holy Spirit. Hence, the reference to the word *spirit*. Whereas previously our minds have been dominated and controlled by Satan's lies and deceptions, now we must expose our minds to the Holy Spirit, the spirit of truth, who brings to us the truth of God.

> And do not be conformed to this world, but be transformed by the renewing of your mind, so that you may prove what the will of God is, that which is good and acceptable and perfect.
>
> Romans 12:2, NASB

Paul instructs us not to be conformed to this world—that is, not to let the old self have his way in our lives. Instead, we are to be transformed, to find out the will of God, which is the development and maturing of the new self. Both in Ephesians 4 and Romans 12, Paul asserts that this one essential phase in the process of cultivating the new self is the renewing of our minds, a work of the Holy Spirit. Paul, in praying for the Ephesian Christians, describes further what needs to happen: "I pray that the eyes of your heart may be enlightened, so that you will know what is the hope of His calling" (Ephesians 1:18, NASB).

"The hope of His calling" is the full development of the new self. But before we can know that, the eyes of our hearts have to be enlightened by the Holy Spirit. The implication is that our hearts have been in darkness and in ignorance. The Holy Spirit has to bring the light of truth to us. And through the truth, our eyes are enlightened and we can see clearly the calling God has for us in the new man.

The Holy Spirit helps us do that by using Scripture as a type of mirror. James tells us that some people look into the Word of God but then walk away unchanged. Presenting the Word of God to such persons does them no permanent good because though they see their likeness in the mirror, they turn around and walk off and forget what the mirror has shown them and take no appropriate action. The alternative, James says, is to "[look] intently at the perfect law, the law of liberty, and [abide] by it, not having become a forgetful hearer but an effectual doer, this man will be blessed in what he does" (James 1:25, NASB).

The mirror actually shows us the two natures, the two selves. It shows us, first of all, what we are by nature: the old self, the criminal Barabbas, the one whose rightful place is on the cross. And then, if we will accept that verdict, yet believe what God promises, the mirror also shows us what we can become by grace—the new self. This is exactly what Paul is saying in 2 Corinthians 3:18:

> But we all, with unveiled face, beholding as in a mirror [that is the Word] the glory of the Lord, are being transformed into the same image from glory to glory, just as from the Lord, the Spirit.
>
> NASB

Notice the word *transformed* again. Remember that Paul said we have to be transformed by the renewing of our minds. In fact, our minds are renewed as we look in the mirror of the Word of God and see the glory of the Lord. That is the image of what God wants to change us into—the image of God restored in the new self. We see also that this change in us is a process of ongoing victory ("from glory to glory"), and the One who works the process is the Spirit, the Holy Spirit. But He only works in us while we are looking in the mirror of God's Word!

God's Plan for Us

What is God's program for the new man? What is the purpose for which God created the new man? In order to answer and understand these questions, we need to go back to God's original purpose for humankind. Speaking about our place and relationship to God in Christ, Paul says:

> In him [Christ] we were also chosen, having been predestined according to the plan of him who works out everything in conformity with the purpose of his will.
>
> Ephesians 1:11, NIV

That is good news. We discussed in chapter 2 our being foreknown, predestined and chosen as part of our calling. We must understand further that when God establishes His purpose, He never abandons it! We are in line with the plan of our God who works out everything in conformity with the purpose of His will. In the final analysis, everything is going to fall in line with that will. This applies to His original purpose in creating man. Sin and Satan have delayed it, but they will never ultimately prevent it! God is not so concerned about time as we are. In fact, He is extremely patient. It may take many years or centuries, maybe even many ages, but He will always ultimately work out His purpose and His plan.

God's original purpose in creating humankind is stated at the beginning of the Bible:

> Then God said, "Let Us make man in Our image, according to Our likeness; and let them rule over the fish of the sea and over the birds of the sky and over the cattle and over all the earth, and over every creeping thing that creeps on the earth."
>
> Genesis 1:26, NASB

We notice that God speaks about *man* first in the singular and then in the plural. He says, "Let Us make man," and then He says, "Let them rule." In other words, He is talking about His purpose for the whole human race, not just for one individual man.

Two main purposes are revealed in this statement of God. The first is that man is to show forth God's likeness. In the record of Creation given in the opening chapters of Genesis, God created man on the sixth day and then He rested. He had His Sabbath on the seventh day. This brings out the fact that God would not rest until He brought forth His own likeness. Everything else in creation was building up to that one supreme objective—that God should reproduce His own likeness. That, I believe, is equally true in the new creation. God will not rest until He has reproduced His own likeness!

The second purpose for man is to exercise God's authority on His behalf. He said of man, "Let them rule," and then He added, "over all the earth." Man was intended to be God's designated ruler, exercising God's authority on His behalf over all the earth.

Man's sin frustrated both of these purposes that God intended for him. In the first place, God's image in man was marred by sin. Second, man, who was destined to be a ruler, became a slave—the slave of sin and of Satan.

Our Responsibility and Destiny

What is our ultimate responsibility? Remember: God will always work out His purpose and His plan. Romans 8:29 gives us this insight: "For those whom He [God] foreknew, He also predestined to become conformed to the image of His Son, so that He would be the firstborn among many brethren" (NASB).

God's purpose, God's destiny for the new man is, first, to become conformed to the image of His Son that He—the Son, Jesus— might be the firstborn among many brethren. God's plan is to bring forth many children, all of whom reproduce the likeness of God's oldest Son, His firstborn, His only begotten—Jesus. That is our first responsibility in the new creation, in the new self.

Our second responsibility is to exercise Christ's authority on His behalf. After His resurrection, Jesus said to His disciples, "All authority has been given to Me in heaven and on earth. Go therefore and make disciples of all the nations" (Matthew 28:18–19, NASB).

Here is another *therefore*, and we need to see the point. Jesus says, "The authority has been given to Me, but I'm sending you to exercise that authority on My behalf as My delegated representatives." Our responsibility is to exercise Christ's authority on His behalf by making disciples out of all the nations.

This is expressed in two actions Jesus tells us to do. First, baptize them in the name of the Father and the Son and the Holy Spirit (see Matthew 28:19). In other words, when we use the name of the triune God, it indicates that the authority of the triune God is behind all that we do. The next action is to teach them to observe all that Jesus commanded (see verse 20). Our teaching is the expression of the delegated authority of Jesus Christ. We are not commissioned to teach anything that we please; we are commissioned to teach all that Jesus taught His first disciples. This process is to continue until the end of the age, as indicated by Jesus when He says, "Lo, I am with you always, even to the end of the age" (verse 20).

There is one more important fact for us to consider. It is this: These purposes for the new self cannot be fulfilled completely by any individual believer. Instead, their fulfillment requires the collective new man—the Body of Christ. Paul says:

> For he himself [Jesus] is our peace, who has made the two [Jew and Gentile] one and has destroyed the barrier, the dividing wall of hostility, by abolishing in his flesh the law with its commandments and regulations. His purpose was to create in himself one new man out of the two.
>
> Ephesians 2:14–15, NIV

The one new man comprises all the people of God and operates through this collective, corporate Body. Paul explains, "From him [Jesus] the whole body, joined and held together by every supporting ligament, grows and builds itself up in love, as each part does its work" (Ephesians 4:16, NIV).

We are to be one complete corporate Body expressing one new corporate man. This new man reenacts Christ's earthly ministry and in this way fulfills our responsibility: We show God to the world and we exercise God's authority on His behalf.

We cannot fulfill our callings, we cannot advance the Kingdom, we cannot reach our full potential or operate in proper authority until we walk in the freedom of the new self—both individually and corporately. Let's continue with what that freedom means for the collective new man, the Body of Christ.

11

Completing Your Assignment

> The Spirit and the bride say, "Come!"
>
> Revelation 22:17

Very simply, the Body of Christ is the Bride, and we walk in obedience to our callings when we take up what the Spirit says. God's purpose is not fulfilled if it is merely the Spirit who says, "Come," or if it is the preacher who says, "Come." God is waiting for the whole Body to say, "Come." That will happen only when the Spirit has His way with the Bride.

The principle of the Bride is really the climax of human history. It is what all history is building toward—and it is exciting to think that all history is building toward a marriage. Few Christians realize the importance of marriage in the eyes of God. We honor marriage, of course, and we believe in faithfulness, but I do not think we get sufficiently excited about marriage as we should.

Ruth and I wrote a book called *God Is a Matchmaker*, which describes how you can find God's plan for your marriage. The book is not about how to live after you get married, but how to live in such a way that you marry God's appointed mate for you. I believe that God has an appointed mate for every one who is to marry. I have heard Christians say, "God showed me the house I was to live in ... the car I was to buy ... the suit I was to wear." If God does that, surely it is much more important that He show you whom to marry.

I have been married twice. God showed me sovereignly and supernaturally in each of those occasions whom I was to marry. God knows that I am not a good judge of character. (I am rather easily deceived by certain types of people.) So God did not trust me to choose my own bride. He very clearly showed me whom I was to choose, and I am so glad I made the right choice each time.

The Bride's Attire

Human history begins with a marriage, and human history is consummated with a marriage: The Marriage Supper of the Lamb completes the whole purpose of God for His people. If you are not excited about marriage, you are really not in line with God's purposes. The whole universe is going to be excited about it. The praise that we are going to hear on that occasion has never echoed through the universe in that measure before.

> "Let us be glad and rejoice and give Him glory, for the marriage of the Lamb has come, and His wife has made herself ready." And to her it was granted to be arrayed in fine linen, clean and bright, for the fine linen is the righteous acts of the saints.
>
> Revelation 19:7–8

When a woman gets married she is usually very concerned about what clothing she is going to wear for the wedding ceremony. In the many different lands and cultures I have visited, I have always found this to be true. I do not believe that is vanity or worldliness; I believe it is actually pleasing to God.

Concern for her clothing is also true of the Bride of Christ. She is going to be adorned in something special: "fine linen, clean and bright." It is going to be shining attire. The book of Revelation tells us what that clothing will be made of: "the righteous acts of the saints." That tells me that in order for the Bride to be properly clothed—as she must be and as God expects—the Bride, the Church, is going to have to do everything God has appointed for her to do. Otherwise she will not be adequately attired. We must complete every righteous act that God expects of us—not just individually, but corporately as the Body of Christ—before we can be ready for the wedding.

We learned in chapter 4 that when we are saved through faith in Jesus Christ, we receive a gift of righteousness. We do not have to work for it; it is imputed to us. We are clothed with a robe of Christ's righteousness, which is wonderful. But this verse in Revelation is not talking about *imputed* righteousness, a gift given on the basis of faith. It is talking about *outworked* righteousness, righteous acts based upon our individual behavior and responses. These righteous acts are the raiment we are going to wear in eternity.

This is a great motivation to me as I walk in my calling. I am continually exercised that I do not omit any of the righteous acts that God has appointed for me in my ministry. But it goes far beyond each of us personally. It applies to the whole Body of Christ. We, corporately, are going to have to complete all our assignments and fulfill every righteous act before we can be ready for the Marriage Supper of the Lamb. Let's read those words once again: "And to her it was granted to be arrayed [or clothed] in fine linen, clean and bright, for the fine linen is the righteous acts of the saints."

Every righteous act done in faith and obedience is a thread in this linen garment. I wonder whether some Christians are going to have rather skimpy wedding dresses unless they change their ways. It is a very searching thought. Each of us had better give attention; we must complete all the righteous acts assigned to us before the Bride can be ready.

Kingdom Assignments

In order to prepare ourselves for the Marriage Supper of the Lamb, we need to understand the basic nature of what God asks of the Church. The responsibility of the Church relates to our various assignments regarding the Kingdom of God.

When the New Testament speaks about the Gospel, it nearly always calls it "the Gospel of the Kingdom." The Gospel is the Good News that God is going to establish His Kingdom on earth. In relationship to that Good News, we have three primary responsibilities. First of all, we are to proclaim the Good News of the Kingdom. Second, we are to demonstrate the Kingdom in our corporate lives. This means we are to show people—by the way we live and by the way we relate to one another—what the Kingdom of God is like, because the Kingdom of God is already in us. "For the kingdom of God is not eating and drinking, but righteousness and peace and joy in the Holy Spirit" (Romans 14:17).

Without the Holy Spirit, it is impossible to demonstrate the Kingdom. We are obligated, not only individually, but even more corporately, to demonstrate to the whole world the nature of God's Kingdom by our lives—lives of righteousness, peace and joy in the Holy Spirit.

Our third responsibility is to prepare the way for the establishment of God's Kingdom on earth. That is really what I want to deal with for the rest of this chapter, for our highest calling is to be His representatives and align ourselves with the purposes of God. How do we prepare the way for the establishment of God's Kingdom on earth?

How to Prepare the Way

In answer to that question, we will be looking at a series of Scriptures from Matthew's gospel.

Repent and Align

First we must repent of rebellion and align ourselves with God's purpose. "From that time Jesus began to preach and to say, 'Repent, for the kingdom of heaven [God] is at hand'" (Matthew 4:17).

This is Jesus' first message. His first proclamation is "God's Kingdom is on the way. Repent. Lay aside your rebellion, your self-will, your self-pleasing, and be prepared to submit to the King." That is the whole thrust of the Gospel.

Further we read:

> And Jesus went about all Galilee, teaching in their synagogues, preaching the gospel of the kingdom, and healing all kinds of sickness and all kinds of disease among the people. Then His fame went throughout all Syria; and they brought to Him all sick people who were afflicted with various diseases and torments, and those who were demon-possessed, epileptics, and paralytics; and He healed them.
>
> Matthew 4:23–24

God wants us to fulfill His purposes for the Kingdom. You will find that everywhere the Gospel of the Kingdom is spoken of, for example, it is attested by the healing of the sick. Actually, the Kingdom of God and sickness are incompatible. They cannot coexist. Where the Kingdom comes, sickness has to go—whether it is in an individual or in the Church.

Have the Right Priority

How do we have the right priorities for preparing the way for God's Kingdom? First we must always approach God in the proper manner. Look at the prayer that Jesus taught us: "Our Father in heaven, hallowed be Your name. Your kingdom come. Your will be done on earth as it is in heaven" (Matthew 6:9–10).

Having approached God, what is the first petition we make? "Your Kingdom come." Not "Give us our daily bread." Not "Forgive us our trespasses." Not "Deliver us from the evil one." All those are legitimate petitions. But the primary petition is to line up with the purposes of God—"Your Kingdom come. Your will be done." Only when we are aligned with God's purposes are we entitled to make our personal petitions, because until then, we are rebels. "Seek first the kingdom of God and His righteousness, and all these things shall be added to you" (Matthew 6:33). Notice that there is no righteousness apart from the Kingdom. If you are not under the Kingdom, you are a rebel, and no rebel is righteous.

Have you got your priorities in order? Are you seeking first the Kingdom of God? Or is it somewhere down low on your list? Are you more concerned about your own personal needs and desires than you are about God's Kingdom?

I have noticed one thing about people who are under the power of the devil (and I have dealt with hundreds of them). There is one problem they almost all have in common: They are self-centered. That is a prison in which the devil shuts people up. Me. My little problems. My needs. My issues. As long as you are living in your needs, you are not living in the Kingdom. Jesus said to seek first the Kingdom and then "all these things," your material needs, will be supplied.

Do you believe that? I want to tell you that God is not stingy. Sometimes church boards are stingy. Missionary organizations can be stingy. But God is not stingy. If the organization you are serving throws you out or cuts you off, just fall into the hands of the living God. He will take better care of you than most religious organizations.

Demonstrate the Kingdom

Next, we prepare the way with a demonstration of the Kingdom. When Jesus sent the first apostles out, He said, "As you go, preach, saying, 'The kingdom of heaven is at hand.'" And because the Kingdom of heaven is at hand, what is the first thing we do? "Heal the sick, cleanse the lepers, raise the dead, cast out demons" (Matthew 10:7–8). Satan hates these ministries because they are public demonstrations that the Kingdom of God has come.

Know the Opposition

Bear in mind that Satan also has a kingdom.

> But Jesus knew their thoughts, and said to them: "Every kingdom divided against itself is brought to desolation, and every city or house divided against itself will not stand. If Satan casts out Satan, he is divided against himself. How then will his kingdom stand? . . . But if I cast out demons by the Spirit of God, surely the kingdom of God has come upon you."
>
> Matthew 12:25–26, 28

The kingdom of Satan cannot be destroyed and the Kingdom of God cannot be established on earth until the Church has fulfilled her task. That is why Satan, whose supreme ambition is to hold onto his kingdom, does everything he can to deceive and blind the Church. He does this to keep her from her great primary responsibilities, because once she fulfills those responsibilities, he knows his kingdom will come to an end.

Satan really does not get too upset over individual souls being saved. He does not even get very upset over new churches being started. He does not like it, of course, but it is not going to cost him his kingdom. There are two things that are going to cost Satan his kingdom—and they are part of the next mission of the Bride.

Prepare for the End

The two Scriptures that follow tell us what must happen before the end of the world—and the end of Satan's kingdom—can occur:

> And this gospel of the kingdom will be preached in all the world as a witness to all the nations, and then the end will come.
>
> Matthew 24:14

> For I do not desire, brethren, that you should be ignorant of this mystery, lest you should be wise in your own opinion, that blindness in part has happened to Israel until the fullness [full number] of the Gentiles has come in. And so all Israel will be saved, as it is written: "The Deliverer [the Messiah] will come out of Zion."
>
> Romans 11:25–26

In God's program, Jesus cannot come and establish His Kingdom until, first, the Church has preached the Gospel of the Kingdom in all the world, and, second, the full number of the Gentiles has come in and Israel has been reconciled to their God through the Messiah. Those are the two things that Satan opposes with all his power, malice and cunning. Most of the religious activities we engage in do not trouble him in the least bit. He is perfectly content.

His kingdom can coexist with most church Christianity. But these two things he fears and fights—the Gospel of the Kingdom being proclaimed in all the world to all nations, and the reconciliation of Israel.

If you live in the Middle East you live in a furnace, because that is where the consummation of the age is going to come. All the forces of evil are mustering in that little area of territory at the east end of the Mediterranean because Satan knows as long as he can keep his hold on Israel, his kingdom is safe.

All of us—individually and corporately—need to take seriously the mandate given to the Bride. As we find God's calling for our lives, individually and corporately, and live to fulfill it, we will be preparing the way for the Kingdom of God on earth. We will be taking our part in the fulfillment of the prayer Jesus taught us to pray— "Thy kingdom come"—for it will usher in the King! The return of Jesus Christ is the subject of our next chapter.

12

The Hope of Your Calling

Then the glory of the LORD will be revealed, and all flesh will see it together; for the mouth of the LORD has spoken.

Isaiah 40:5, NASB

One of the major issues in the minds of many Christians is eschatology. In this chapter, we will discuss what our attitude should be toward the coming of the Lord as it relates to our calling in Christ.

Eschatology, as you probably know, means "the study of what is going to happen at the end of the age." I will tell you frankly that there are a lot of events that are going to happen at the end of the age that I know nothing about. My eschatology has some cracks in it. But that does not keep me from facing objective facts. I was trained to analyze the meaning of words. No matter what my preconceptions may be, I try to find out what the Bible is really saying. And it is usually saying something different from what I expect it to say.

The Early Church: Watching and Waiting

Let's begin by addressing the attitude of the early Christians toward the return of the Lord. I am not sure I know what their eschatology was, but I venture to suggest to you that if we take the words of the New Testament to mean what they say, the Church lived in excited anticipation of the Lord's return.

We are going to look at a number of passages from the major epistles in the New Testament, and I could easily double the number, but I think you will get the picture. We start with Paul's letter to the Corinthians:

> Therefore you do not lack any spiritual gift as you eagerly wait for our Lord Jesus Christ to be revealed. He will keep you strong to the end, so that you will be blameless on the day of our Lord Jesus Christ.
>
> 1 Corinthians 1:7–8, NIV

The Corinthian church was eagerly waiting for the Lord Jesus to be revealed, and Paul promised them that Jesus would keep them strong until that day. There is no doubt in my mind that they were very much looking forward to that day.

Then in 1 Corinthians 11, in the ordinance for the Lord's Supper, let's look at just one verse: "For whenever you eat this bread and drink this cup, you proclaim the Lord's death until he comes" (1 Corinthians 11:26, NIV).

According to that ordinance, which Paul claims was given him by direct revelation from the Lord Jesus Christ, every time we take the Lord's Supper (Holy Communion or the Eucharist), we are looking forward to His return. I once read a beautiful comment on that verse. It said that when we take Communion, everything of secondary importance drops out of sight. There is no past but the cross, no future but the coming. We show the Lord's death till He comes. I believe that is a right perspective. One of the benefits of Communion should be that it always restores that perspective of the coming of the Lord.

Next we look at a number of verses from Paul's letter to the Thessalonians:

> May he [God] strengthen your hearts so that you will be blameless and holy in the presence of our God and Father when our Lord Jesus comes with all his holy ones.
>
> 1 Thessalonians 3:13, NIV

These Thessalonian Christians were looking forward and preparing themselves to be blameless and holy for the Lord's return. Further on in the same epistle, we read:

> According to the Lord's own word, we tell you that we who are still alive, who are left till the coming of the Lord, will certainly not precede those who have fallen asleep.
>
> 1 Thessalonians 4:15, NIV

Again, the great anticipated event is the coming of the Lord. And then a little further on in the same epistle, we find these words:

> May God himself, the God of peace, sanctify you through and through. May your whole spirit, soul and body be kept blameless at the coming of our Lord Jesus Christ.
>
> 1 Thessalonians 5:23, NIV

It seems there was a direct connection between the need for personal holiness and the anticipation of the Lord's return.

Next, let's look at some passages in Paul's letters to Timothy:

> In the sight of God, who gives life to everything, and of Christ Jesus, who while testifying before Pontius Pilate made the good confession, I charge you to keep this command without spot or blame until the appearing of our Lord Jesus Christ.
>
> 1 Timothy 6:13–14, NIV

Again, the terminus, the point to which they were looking, the challenge to be faithful, is the coming of our Lord Jesus Christ. Then we find a rather similar challenge and a very solemn one to those of us who are preachers:

> In the presence of God and of Christ Jesus, who will judge
> the living and the dead, and in view of his appearing and his
> kingdom, I give you this charge: Preach the Word.
>
> 2 Timothy 4:1–2, NIV

In the same epistle, a little later in the same chapter, Paul
wrote:

> Now there is in store for me the crown of righteousness, which
> the Lord, the righteous Judge, will award to me on that day—
> and not only to me, but also to all who have longed for his
> appearing.
>
> 2 Timothy 4:8, NIV

The one necessary qualification for receiving the crown of righteousness seems to be that we have longed for His appearance.
Paul writes this to Titus:

> For the grace of God that brings salvation has appeared to
> all men. It teaches us to say "No" to [or deny] ungodliness
> and worldly passions, and to live self-controlled, upright and
> godly lives in this present age, while we wait for the blessed
> hope—the glorious appearing of our great God and Savior,
> Jesus Christ.
>
> Titus 2:11–13, NIV

Again, we see a close connection between holiness and waiting
for the Lord's appearing. We might draw the conclusion that the
"glorious appearing" of Jesus Christ was their primary motivation
for godly living.

Next let's take a look at what James says in his epistle:

> Be patient, then, brothers, until the Lord's coming. See how
> the farmer waits for the land to yield its valuable crop and
> how patient he is for the autumn and spring rains. You too,
> be patient and stand firm, because the Lord's coming is near.
>
> James 5:7–8, NIV

The Lord's coming also seems to be motivation for endurance and holding out.

The apostle Peter speaks about us as Christians:

> Who through faith are shielded by God's power until the coming of the salvation that is ready to be revealed in the last time. In this you greatly rejoice, though now for a little while you may have had to suffer grief in all kinds of trials. These have come so that your faith—of greater worth than gold, which perishes even though refined by fire—may be proved genuine and may result in praise, glory and honor when Jesus Christ is revealed.... Therefore, prepare your minds for action; be self-controlled; set your hope fully on the grace to be given you when Jesus Christ is revealed.
>
> 1 Peter 1:5–7, 13, NIV

Again, my impression is that Christ's coming was the primary motive for right living.

Finally, we will look at John's first epistle: "And now, dear children, continue in him, so that when he appears we may be confident and unashamed before him at his coming" (1 John 2:28, NIV).

Simply as a student of language, I have to say, no matter what view I may have about eschatology, one fact is clear. It is a fact attested to by all the major writers of New Testament epistles. It is this: The supreme anticipation of New Testament Christians was the coming of the Lord. It encouraged them to strive to be blameless and holy. It was the main qualification for receiving the crown of righteousness. It helped them endure. It was their motive for right living. They lived with their eyes toward that event.

The Lord once gave me an interpretation of a message that was brought forth in a public meeting. One of the things He said was this: *The natural mind of man has no way to calculate how close the coming of the Lord may be.* As far as I am concerned, that is absolutely correct. I do not believe any of us has a way to calculate. But I believe all of us should have the same anticipation that the New Testament Church had.

141

Sometimes our theories get in the way of the facts. You may never have had the experience of having a pain that no doctor can diagnose. While I was in the British army, I had a tremendous pain in my rib for six weeks. Because I was with an infantry unit at the time and life was pretty hectic, it was agony for me to do all the duties I was required to do. When I went to the doctor and told him about my pain, he put his stethoscope on me, but could not hear anything. Then they put me through every conceivable test available at that time and came to the conclusion there was no reason for my pain. The implication was, "You don't really have a pain!" Well, I knew better. I had a pain, whether they could diagnose it or not.

Using that as an example, we make our statement again. Whether our eschatology makes room for it or not, the fact is that the New Testament Church lived in anticipation of the Lord's return. As far as I am concerned, whether it suits me or not, that is a fact.

The New Lifestyle

If this was the view of the Early Church, should it not be a primary focus for us as well? It is a lifestyle I have glimpsed and at times have tasted. I cannot say it is entirely possible actually to live this way, but I feel it is where we ought to be headed.

There are two aspects to this lifestyle, and both are part of whatever specific calling God has placed on your life. First of all, the main motivation of your lifestyle and calling ought to be to bring the Gospel to the ends of the earth. I believe I can honestly say that I will never be satisfied until that has been achieved. Whatever part God has given me in it is secondary, but that is the only legitimate motivation. Second, a main expectation of your lifestyle and calling ought to be the return of Christ.

Could you be that kind of person? A person who lives with one main motivation—to reach the ends of the earth with the Gospel. A person who has one expectation—the coming of the Lord. The lifestyle of people like this is distinctive. They are a different kind of people. I have moved among them and, in fact, at times I have been on that level. Once you have tasted it, you will never be satisfied with less.

This way of living does not make sense by worldly or religious standards. As I have studied the background and the history of the emergence of the State of Israel, I have been tremendously challenged. I felt I had to study this to some extent because of my calling. David Ben-Gurion was one of the early Zionists and the first prime minister of Israel, way back in the days when Zionism was regarded as some kind of silly fad that a few people entertained. Zionism was scoffed at and rejected, even by the majority of Jewish people. And the world dismissed it as both impossible and ridiculous. Ben-Gurion himself said, "To be a Zionist, you have to be crazy."

That is the kind of lifestyle I am talking about. To live it you have to be crazy. When I look back at the State of Israel what I see is that their craziness paid off. You have no idea unless you study the literature back in those days between World War I and World War II how many "experts" contemptuously dismissed any possibility of the emergence of the State of Israel. In the 1911 edition of the *Encyclopedia Britannica*, which is one of the major learned works of our civilization, a certain German professor was discussing the possibility of ever accurately recovering the pronunciation of ancient Hebrew. And he said, "That possibility is as remote as the possibility that a Jewish empire will ever be established again in the Middle East." That was published in 1911 by the experts. Thirty-seven years later the experts were looking very silly.

If we are going to live in the way I described above, we are going to become the target of the experts—both religious and worldly. When I consider the tasks that Zionists took on at that time it is amazing, considering that the British were the mandatory power governing Palestine, which is now Israel. They were undoubtedly the largest and most powerful empire in the world and one of the most powerful in human history. A little group of Zionist nobodies from many diverse backgrounds in essence challenged the British Empire. And they won! To me, this is a beautiful word of encouragement, regardless of what your attitude is toward the State of Israel. What I am saying is, let's be a little bit crazy.

I believe I can say this confidently, hoping that you know I have both feet on the ground. I am not some kind of weird fanatic. I am not overly emotional. I am a balanced personality. And as some of my close friends have been so kind to say, I have fruit to prove it. But I am not satisfied with myself. Let me say it that way. I am afraid sometimes that I am getting too respectable. (Some who know me see no danger of that!) I want to live in a radical way. I want to go out and challenge Goliath. Even though I may have only five stones in my sling, I am prepared to take him on. And do you know what I believe? I believe we are going to win.

In fact, I have looked at the end of the Book—and we *do* win.

13

A Kingdom of Priests

Therefore, holy brethren, partakers of the heavenly calling, consider the Apostle and High Priest of our confession, Christ Jesus, who was faithful to Him who appointed Him.

Hebrews 3:1–2

What is the practical outworking of our identification with Jesus in our daily living as believers or as disciples? How does it affect the way we live? What kind of people should we be?

I consider the Scripture below to be not only one of the most exciting, but also one of the most challenging statements of the New Testament. This statement is found in the gospel of John. It details the first appearance of Jesus after His resurrection to His disciples collectively in a group, which took place on the evening of the Sunday of the resurrection. The disciples were shut away in a locked room for fear of the Jews and suddenly Jesus was right there in their midst. This is what happened:

On the evening of that first day of the week, when the disciples were together, with the doors locked for fear of the Jews, Jesus came and stood among them and said, "Peace be with you!" After he said this, he showed them his hands and side [to prove to them that He was the very same Person they had seen hanging on the cross]. The disciples were overjoyed when they saw the Lord. Again Jesus said, "Peace be with you! As the Father has sent me, I am sending you." And with that he breathed on them and said, "Receive the Holy Spirit."

John 20:19–22, NIV

Undoubtedly, the disciples' hearts were pounding so much that I am sure they needed the repetition of that message of peace (which is still a typical Middle Eastern greeting, by the way). They were half fearful, half afraid. They could scarcely believe what was happening. The next words Jesus spoke are the ones I want to focus on: "As the Father has sent me, I am sending you." Then through that inbreathed breath of the resurrected Christ, the Holy Spirit entered into each of those disciples in a totally new way. Through the Holy Spirit, the very life and nature of Jesus was imparted to them. On the basis of that impartation of His own life and nature, Jesus was able to say to them those astonishing words—that He was sending them forth.

The Father sent Jesus into the world to fulfill a unique task that no one else could fulfill. Jesus had completed that task and was about to return to the Father. He did not leave Himself without representatives on the earth, however. He said to those disciples, "Just in the same way the Father originally sent Me to fulfill a special task, now, in turn, I am sending you, My disciples, to fulfill a special task. I will be returning to the Father, but I'll be leaving you on earth as My representatives."

What is included in the phrase "just as the Father sent Me"? Let's turn to an earlier passage in John's gospel to provide some answers to that question. In John 14, Philip is talking to Jesus:

Philip said, "Lord, show us the Father and that will be enough for us." Jesus answered: "Don't you know me, Philip, even after I have been among you such a long time? Anyone who has seen me has see the Father. How can you say, 'Show us the Father'? Don't you believe that I am in the Father, and

that the Father is in me? The words I say to you are not just
my own. Rather, it is the Father, living in me, who is doing
his work."

John 14:8–10, NIV

Jesus' response to Philip brings up three aspects of the relationship
of Jesus with the Father. First of all, Jesus did not speak His own
words. He spoke words that had been committed to Him to speak
by the Father who sent Him. Second, Jesus did not do anything
in His miraculous ministry through His own power or ability. He
said, "Really, I'm not doing it. It's the Father who is performing
His works through Me." Third—and this is even more amazing—to
see Jesus was to see the Father. He said, "You don't need to see the
Father. You've seen Me. And if you've seen Me, you've seen the
Father."

Let me summarize. First, Jesus spoke words proceeding from
the Father. Second, the Father performed His works through Jesus.
Third, to see Jesus was to see the Father.

Here is the application. Jesus said, "Just as the Father sent Me,
I'm sending you." In other words, "The relationship that existed
between the Father and Me will be the same relationship that exists
between Me and you, My disciples."

What does that mean? It means that exactly what was true of the
relationship of Jesus to the Father should be true of our relationship
to Jesus. First of all, we do not speak our own words; we speak words
proceeding from Jesus. Second, we do not do our own works. It is
Jesus in us performing His works, just as it was the Father in Jesus
performing His works. Third, to see us is to see Jesus. Isn't that a
challenge and a responsibility?

We are Christ's official representatives here on earth, each with
a specific assignment to perform. This same truth is beautifully presented by Paul in 2 Corinthians:

> Therefore, if anyone is in Christ, he is a new creation; the
> old has gone, the new has come! All this is from God, who
> reconciled us to himself through Christ and gave us the min-
> istry of reconciliation: that God was reconciling the world

147

to himself in Christ, not counting men's sins against them. And he has committed to us the message of reconciliation. We are therefore Christ's ambassadors, as though God were making his appeal through us. We implore you on Christ's behalf: Be reconciled to God. God made him [Jesus] who had no sin to be sin for us, so that in him we might become the righteousness of God.

2 Corinthians 5:17–21, NIV

This process starts with a new creation. This is the ultimate in passing out of death into a new life. Then, in that new creation we become the official representatives of God and of Christ on the earth. Just as God was in Christ reconciling the world to Himself, so now Christ is in us reconciling the world to God. We are Christ's ambassadors, Paul says, as though God were making His appeal through us to be reconciled to Him. That total identification with Jesus is the only basis for reconciliation. And so the closing verse says, "God made him [Jesus] who had no sin to be sin for us, so that in him we might become the righteousness of God" (verse 21, NIV).

Notice two essential points. First, we cannot become Christ's representatives until we have first been transformed ourselves. We must enter into the new creation. We must be created anew. The old creation has no message.

Second, let me emphasize once again that our message is based on that divine exchange that took place at the cross. There at Calvary, God made Jesus, who had no sin, to be sin for us that we might become the righteousness of God in Him. Think of yourself as a reconciled reconciler. First, you have to be reconciled to God through Christ. Then you become God's agent and messenger of reconciliation through Christ to the rest of this world.

Kings and Priests

Let's now take this process one step further. We are identified not only with the resurrection life and ministry of Jesus, but also with His ascension life and ministry in heaven. When Jesus ascended to heaven and took His place on the throne with the Father, He entered into His two supreme, unique and final ministries. He became King and Priest. In this also, we are invited to identify ourselves with Jesus.

A number of passages from the book of Revelation express this truth very well:

> To him who loves us and has freed us from our sins by his blood, and has made us to be a kingdom and priests to serve his God and Father—to him be glory and power for ever and ever! Amen.
>
> Revelation 1:5–6, NIV

Notice that when Jesus has freed us from our sin by His own blood, it is by that very act that He has made us to be a kingdom and priests (or kings and priests, or a kingdom of priests) to God and the Father.

The same truth is brought out again in Revelation 5:

> And they sang a new song: "You [Jesus] are worthy to take the scroll and to open its seals, because you were slain, and with your blood you purchased men for God from every tribe and language and people and nation. You have made them to be a kingdom and priests to serve our God, and they will reign on the earth."
>
> Revelation 5:9–10, NIV

Notice that when we are purchased or redeemed by the blood of Jesus, it is through that purchase that we are made to be a kingdom and priests to God.

In writing to believers in his first epistle, Peter states this as well: "But you are a chosen people, a royal priesthood [or a kingly priesthood]" (1 Peter 2:9, NIV). What are the particular, special responsibilities of kings and priests? It should be fairly clear to us that the responsibility or task of a king is to rule. Many people do not see as clearly the task of a priest, but it is made clear in Scripture. The responsibility of priests is to offer sacrifices. In God's order,

149

only priests could offer sacrifices to God. So we are made kings to rule and priests to offer sacrifices.

With regard to our offering sacrifices as priests, I quote another passage from 1 Peter: "You also, like living stones, are being built into a spiritual house to be a holy priesthood, offering spiritual sacrifices acceptable to God through Jesus Christ" (1 Peter 2:5, NIV).

The moment we are called a holy priesthood, it follows that we must have sacrifices to offer to God. Peter says that these are "spiritual sacrifices." In other words, they are not like the sacrifices of the Mosaic Law. They are not animals. In particular we follow the example of Jesus, who in heaven offers to God the spiritual sacrifice of His intercession and prayer on our behalf. Scripture clearly tells us, "He is also able to save to the uttermost those who come to God through Him, since He always lives to make intercession for them" (Hebrews 7:25).

Jesus' earthly ministry lasted only three and a half years, but His ministry as a King and a Priest has already lasted nearly two thousand years. And that ministry of Jesus will continue to go on throughout eternity. We are invited not only to share with Jesus His earthly ministry, but through our identification with Him, also to enter His eternal, heavenly ministry as kings and priests. Spiritually, our identification with Jesus already makes us citizens of the heavenly Zion. This is not something that has yet to happen—it is something that has already taken place through our identification with Jesus.

Wherever you are right now—in your kitchen, in your favorite easy chair, in your living room, at your desk—that is your earthly location. That is the location of your body. You may not realize it, but your spirit has another location. Your spirit is with Jesus. Your spirit is on the throne in Him. You have already come to Mount Zion—the heavenly Zion.

This is so beautifully stated in Hebrews 12. Notice the tenses as we look at this significant passage:

> But you have come to Mount Zion, to the heavenly Jerusalem, the city of the living God. You have come to thousands upon

thousands of angels in joyful assembly, to the church of the firstborn, whose names are written in heaven. You have come to God, the judge of all men, to the spirits of righteous men made perfect, to Jesus the mediator of a new covenant, and to the sprinkled blood that speaks a better word than the blood of Abel.

Hebrews 12:22–24, NIV

This is written to believers on earth, and it does not say "you are going to come"—it says "you *have* come to Mount Zion." That passage describes our spiritual location. Not only is there a great assembly of angels, but the true Church is there in spirit—the Church of the firstborn (all of those who have been born again out of death into a new creation through faith in Jesus Christ). We are already there in that glorious assembly. Out of the heavenly Zion, through our identification with Jesus, we rule on God's behalf through our prayers. We are a kingdom of priests. We rule through prayer. This is stated in Psalm 110:

The LORD says to my Lord: "Sit at my right hand until I make your enemies a footstool for your feet." The LORD will extend your mighty scepter from Zion; you will rule in the midst of your enemies.

Psalm 110:1–2, NIV

Jesus is already ruling, although His enemies are still present. The rod of authority is placed in the hands of God's people as they take their place in Zion. And out of Zion the rod of authority goes forth over the nations of the earth. We are thus identified with Jesus, even now, in His two great final ministries as King and Priest. And that is the amazing culmination of all aspects of our calling in Christ Jesus.

Will You Commit Yourself?

We began this book, Called to Conquer, with the basic principles of how Jesus Christ calls each of us to serve Him in His purposes for us. We have studied the attributes of an authentic calling in God and what it can mean in our lives. In this final chapter, we have learned that the culmination and ultimate goal of our calling is to be identified with Jesus Christ in His ministry as both King and Priest. We are to rule with Him, and we are to intercede with Him. Truly, we have been called to conquer—through victorious service for Jesus Christ until He returns.

Now we have reached the point of commitment. Are you ready to commit yourself fully to Jesus Christ and to the calling He has for you?

Some years ago, I made a promise to the Lord. I said, "God, with Your help, I'll stop delivering religious lectures. When I preach or write on a subject, I will always give people an opportunity to experience what I have preached or written about, if it is practical." Right now, as you finish this final chapter, I am going to give you that opportunity.

Here is the key question: What place does Jesus Christ have in your life? The Church has one Lord. It is Jesus. The Church has one Head. It is Jesus. As far as I am concerned, I belong to the Lord Jesus Christ—spirit, soul and body, for time and eternity. He redeemed me by His blood when He died on the cross, and I have given myself to Him.

Can you say the same? If you cannot, would you make that decision today? Your calling in God is just ahead of you. Will you step into it?

Now Is the Time

I believe we should close this book with an opportunity for you to make a total dedication of your life to the Lord Jesus Christ. That does not mean you are never going to sin again or you are never going to have problems or you are never going to fail. It simply means that you are making a genuine commitment to Jesus Christ, the Lord of the harvest, to be a laborer in the harvest fields. You do not have to go out and resign your job tomorrow or sell your furniture or give up your home. When you commit to Jesus Christ, He will be the One to tell you the next move. But when you are committed to your calling in Jesus Christ, life is rich, life is full. It is exciting and fascinating.

Maybe you are coming to the end of this book somewhat perplexed, confused and uncertain. There may not be in you that deep, settled peace and stability in your Christian experience. The reason it may not be there could well be your lack of total commitment.

Are you prepared to make a definite commitment to Jesus Christ—to follow Him for the rest of time and for all eternity? Are you ready to place your life at His disposal, for Him to use you for His glory in whatever way He wants? If that is your desire, say to Jesus right now, "Lord, I want to give myself totally to You."

A Prayer of Commitment

If you have said those words to Jesus, you are ready to pray the following prayer. First take a moment just to be quiet in the presence of God. When you have finished praying, just turn loose and release yourself to the Lord. Worship Him, praise Him and thank Him.

Please pray this prayer now:

Father, in the name of Jesus I come to You. I love You, Lord, and I thank You for this opportunity to consecrate my life completely to Jesus Christ.

Lord, I stand in my authority as a believer in Jesus Christ, and I loose myself now from every bond, every fetter, from anything that would hold me back from full commitment to Jesus. I declare myself released in the name of Jesus, and I put myself into Your hands, Lord. I place myself at Your disposal. You are the Head over all things to the Church which is Your Body, and I am part of that Body.

Lord, from this moment onward, I place myself under Your control. I believe that You are going to bless me and strengthen me and use me as I commit myself to You and answer Your call upon my life.

Lord, I pray for the harvest. You directed us to ask You, the Lord of the harvest, to send forth laborers into Your harvest. Lord, I present myself to You as one of those laborers. According to Your will for me, as You see fit in my circumstances, my situation and my gifting, please thrust me forth into the harvest field to be a laborer for You, Lord.

I respond wholeheartedly to Your calling on my life, and I now commit myself fully to that calling and to You. In Jesus' name, Amen.

If you just prayed that prayer, you can rejoice in full, knowing that the Lord has heard you, accepted your promise and commissioned you in His service.

May the Lord bless you and fulfill you as you serve Him from this moment onward, knowing with all your heart that you are called to conquer. Your life will never be the same.

Index

ABOUT THE AUTHOR

Derek Prince (1915–2003) was born in India of British parents. He was educated as a scholar of Greek and Latin at Eton College and King's College, Cambridge, in England. Upon graduation he held a fellowship (equivalent to a professorship) in Ancient and Modern Philosophy at King's College. He also studied Hebrew, Aramaic and modern languages at Cambridge and the Hebrew University in Jerusalem. As a student, he was a philosopher and self-proclaimed agnostic.

While in the British Medical Corps during World War II, Derek began to study the Bible as a philosophical work. Converted through a powerful encounter with Jesus Christ, he was baptized in the Holy Spirit a few days later. Out of this encounter, he formed two conclusions: first, that Jesus Christ is alive; second, that the Bible is a true, relevant, up-to-date book. These conclusions altered the whole course of his life, which he then devoted to studying and teaching the Bible as the Word of God.

Discharged from the army in Jerusalem in 1945, he married Lydia Christensen, founder of a children's home there. Upon their marriage, he immediately became father to Lydia's eight adopted daughters—six Jewish, one Palestinian Arab and one English. Together, the family saw the rebirth of the State of Israel in 1948. In the late 1950s, they adopted another daughter while Derek was serving as principal of a teacher training college in Kenya.

In 1963, the Princes immigrated to the United States and pastored a church in Seattle. In 1973, Derek became one of the founders of Intercessors for America. His book *Shaping History through Prayer and Fasting* has awakened Christians around the world to their responsibility to pray for their governments. Many consider underground translations of the book as instrumental in the fall of Communist regimes in the USSR, East Germany and Czechoslovakia.

Lydia Prince died in 1975, and Derek married Ruth Baker (a single mother to three adopted children) in 1978. He met his second wife, like his first wife, while she was serving the Lord in Jerusalem. Ruth died in December 1998 in Jerusalem, where they had lived since 1981.

Until a few years before his own death in 2003 at the age of 88, Derek persisted in the ministry God had called him to as he traveled the world, imparting God's revealed truth, praying for the sick and afflicted and sharing his prophetic insights into world events in the light of Scripture. Internationally recognized as a Bible scholar and spiritual patriarch, he established a teaching ministry that spanned six continents and more than sixty years. He is the author of more than fifty books, six hundred audio teachings and one hundred video teachings, many of which have been translated and published in more than one hundred languages. He pioneered teaching on such groundbreaking themes as generational curses, the biblical significance of Israel and demonology.

Derek's radio program, which began in 1979, has been translated into more than a dozen languages and continues to touch lives. His main gift of explaining the Bible and its teaching in a clear and simple way has helped build a foundation of faith in millions of lives. Derek's nondenominational, nonsectarian approach has made his teaching equally relevant and helpful to people from all racial and religious backgrounds, and his teaching is estimated to have reached more than half the globe.

In 2002, Derek said, "It is my desire—and I believe the Lord's desire—that this ministry continue the work, which God began through me more than sixty years ago, until Jesus returns."

Derek Prince Ministries continues to distribute his teachings and to train missionaries, church leaders and congregations through the outreaches of more than thirty DPM offices around the world, including primary work in Australia, Canada, China, France, Germany, the Netherlands, New Zealand, Norway, Russia, South Africa, Switzerland, the United Kingdom and the United States. For current information about these and other worldwide locations, visit www.derekprince.com.

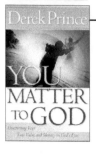
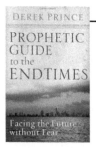

DEREK PRINCE MINISTRIES
WORLDWIDE OFFICES

DPM–ASIA/ PACIFIC
38 Hawdon Street, Sydenham
Christchurch 8023,
New Zealand
Tel: + 64 3 366 4443
E-mail: admin@dpm.co.nz
Web: www.dpm.co.nz and
www.derekprince.in

DPM–AUSTRALIA
1st Floor, 134 Pendle Way
Pendle Hill,
New South Wales 2145,
Australia
Tel: + 612 9688 4488
Email: enquiries@derekprince.com.au
Web: www.derekprince.com.au

DPM–CANADA
P. O. Box 8354 Halifax,
Nova Scotia B3K 5M1,
Canada
Tel: + 1 902 443 9577
E-mail: enquiries.dpm@eastlink.ca
Web: www.derekprince.org

DPM–FRANCE
B.P. 31, Route d'Oupia,
34210 Olonzac,
France
Tel: + 33 468 913872
Email: info@derekprince.fr
Web: www.derekprince.fr

DPM–GERMANY
Schwarzauer Str. 56,
D-83308 Trostberg,
Germany
Tel: + 49 8621 64146
E-mail: IBL.de@t-online.de
Web: www.ibl-dpm.net

DPM–NETHERLANDS
Postbus 326
7100 AH Winterswijk
The Netherlands
Tel: + 31 251 255 044
E-mail: info@nl.derekprince.com
Web: www.dpmnederland.nl

DPM–NORWAY
P. O. Box 129 Lodderfjord
N-5881, Bergen,
Norway
Tel: +47 928 39855
E-mail: sverre@derekprince.no
Web: www.derekprince.no

SINGAPORE
Derek Prince Publications Pte. Ltd.
P. O. Box 2046 ,
Robinson Road Post Office
Singapore 904046
Tel: + 65 6392 1812
E-mail: dpmchina@singnet.com.sg
English web: www.dpmchina.org
Chinese web: www.ygmweb.org

DPM–SOUTH AFRICA
P. O. Box 33367, Glenstantia 0010
Pretoria ,
South Africa
Tel: +27 12 348 9537
E-mail: enquiries@derekprince.co.za
Web: www.derekprince.co.za

DPM–SWITZERLAND
Alpenblick 8 ,
CH-8934 Knonau
Switzerland
Tel: + 41(0) 44 768 25 06
E-mail: dpm-ch@ibl-dpm.net
Web: www.ibl-dpm.net

DPM–UK
Kingsfield, Hadrian Way
Baldock SG7 6AN
UK
Tel: + 44 (0) 1462 492100
Email: enquiries@dpmuk.org
Web: www.dpmuk.org

DPM–USA
P. O. Box 19501
Charlotte NC 28219
USA
Tel: + 1 704 357 3556
E-mail: ContactUs@derekprince.org
Web: www.derekprince.org

Ingram Content Group UK Ltd.
Milton Keynes UK
UKHW022233140323
418546UK00010B/200